TRANSFORMED
by GOD'S
WORD

"This skillful melding of lectio and visio divina helps the reader personally engage God's Word and be shaped by its power. Prepare to be blessed!"

Sarah Christmyer

Codeveloper and author of the Great Adventure Catholic Bible Study Program

"Stephen Binz has artfully combined his scholarship and love of icons to create a book that helps readers enter into the crucial scenes that narrate the life of Jesus. The six-movement process he provides is a guide for prayer and an invitation to encounter Christ who is the focus of the story presented in words and icons. A welcome way to enter into the Good News."

Cackie Upchurch

Director of the Little Rock Scripture Study

"Skillfully uniting icons and scripture, Stephen Binz's meditations invite us toward wholeness and holiness, to hear with the heart's ear and see with the heart's eye."

Aidan Hart

Author of *Icons in the Modern World*

"As one who both practices and teaches visio divina, I highly recommend this book that beautifully links art, prayer, and the healing power of both."

Br. Mickey McGrath, O.S.F.S.

BeeStill Studios

TRANSFORMED
by GOD'S
WORD

Discovering the Power *of*
Lectio *and* Visio Divina

STEPHEN J. BINZ
Icons by Ruta and Kaspars Poikans

AVE MARIA PRESS AVE Notre Dame, Indiana

Founded in 1865, Ave Maria Press is a ministry of the United States Province of Holy Cross.

www.avemariapress.com

Paperback: ISBN-13 978-1-59471-651-5

E-book: ISBN-13 978-1-59471-652-2

Cover image © Ruta and Kaspars Poikans.

Cover and text design by David Scholtes.

Printed and bound in the United States of America.

Library of Congress Cataloging-in-Publication Data
Names: Binz, Stephen J., 1955-
Title: Transformed by God's word : discovering the power of Lectio and Visio divina / Stephen J. Binz ; icons by Ruta and Kaspars Poikans.
Description: Notre Dame, Indiana : Ave Maria Press, 2016.
Identifiers: LCCN 2015039210। ISBN 9781594716515 (pbk.) । ISBN 9781594716522 (e-book)
Subjects: LCSH: Bible. Gospels--Meditations. । Bible. Gospels--Prayers. । Bible. Gospels--Reading. । Bible. Gospels--Devotional use. । Bible. Gospels--Illustrations. । Icons--Cult. । Bible--Reading. । Bible--Devotional use.
Classification: LCC BS2555.54 .B54 2016 । DDC 248.3--dc23
LC record available at http://lccn.loc.gov/2015039210

Contents

Preface

Through my dedication to biblical studies, I grew to appreciate the rich tradition of lectio divina (sacred reading), an ancient way of experiencing scripture as the Word of God. Then though my work in leading pilgrimages to the lands of the Bible, I began to understand the ways in which both sacred texts and sacred images express God's living word.

The places where the events of salvation occurred form what many have described as a "fifth gospel." At these locations the early Christians erected shrines and churches to honor the holy places, and at these sites they experienced the saving events in divine liturgy. In the Church's earliest period, Christians expressed the living Word of God, which they had experienced most fully in Jesus Christ, through both text and image. In both the sacred text and the sacred image, the hearer and the viewer encounter God's saving action and are formed by it into the image of Christ.

I experienced this transforming power of God's word in a wonderful way in the town of Nazareth in Galilee. At the heart of the Basilica of the Annunciation, I gazed into the small cave where Mary experienced the annunciation, a place that has been remembered and honored by the relatives and disciples of Jesus from the earliest times. Under the altar are the words *Verbum caro hic factum est* ("Here the Word became flesh"). In the womb of Mary, the Word became incarnate, and the entire basilica is devoted to honoring this saving mystery through visual arts.

Close to the basilica stands the Mary of Nazareth International Center, which offers services to pilgrims and visitors to Nazareth, including an archaeological site from the first century and a multimedia presentation focusing on Mary within the history of salvation. The center is run by the Chemin Neuf Community, a Catholic community with an ecumenical vocation dedicated to working for unity in Christ's Church and peace in the world.

The Mary of Nazareth International Center is crowned by its Unity Chapel. This quiet space provides an ideal setting for quiet meditation and communal prayer with a view of the basilica and the town of Nazareth. Highlighting this chapel are the twenty icons that are reproduced in this book and the frescos that form the dome. The design and images, produced by Kaspars and Ruta Poikans, express the entire story of the Incarnation.

Ruta and Kaspars Poikans are from Riga, Latvia, where they studied at Riga's Fine Arts Academy and School of Applied Arts. They later studied icon painting in Russia at the Mirozka Monastery in Pskov. Since 1999 they have lived in France, where they joined the Communauté du Chemin Neuf. In their Saint Luke Workshop within Notre Dame des Dombes Abbey, Kaspars and Ruta make icons, frescoes, mosaics, sculptures, and liturgical furnishings. They have created the icons featured within this book and continue to fashion sacred visual art in France and throughout the world.

I have discovered that the tradition of meditative reading of scripture and that of meditative gazing through icons can lead Christians to a fuller experience of God's living word. Joining the rich traditions of Western and Eastern Christianity, this holistic experience of God's word encourages the Church, as the Body of Christ, to breathe deeply with both of its lungs. I pray that this multi-sensory experience of the divine word will lead you more completely into the heart of Jesus Christ.

Learn more about Mary of Nazareth International Center at www.cimdn.org, about Kaspars and Ruta Poikans at www.ateliersaintluc.fr, and about Stephen J. Binz at www.Bridge-B.com.

Stephen J. Binz

The
Ancient Tradition of
Lectio Divina

The theologians and spiritual masters of the ancient Church teach us to ponder the scriptures while asking God to illumine our minds and hearts. They urge us to study and pray the words of the sacred texts as a way of being formed by the Word of God. These early teachers called this practice *lectio divina* ("sacred reading").

Rather than keeping scripture at a safe analytical distance, this formational reading leads us to personally encounter God through the sacred text. It opens us to personal engagement with God's word. We involve ourselves intimately, openly, and receptively through what we read. Our goal is not just to use the text to acquire more knowledge, get advice, or form an opinion about the passage. Rather, the inspired text becomes the subject of our reading relationship and we become the object that is acted upon and shaped by scripture. Reading with expectation, we patiently allow the text to address us, to probe us, and to form us into the image of Jesus Christ.

Formed to Live "In Christ"

Throughout the history of salvation as expressed in scripture, God desires to free us from the many types of bondage that prevent us from living in the divine image. The goal of reading scripture within the Christian life is to form us into the image of Jesus Christ. Through Baptism and the life of faith we begin to live "in Christ." This involves a new way of seeing, a new way of living—indeed, a new identity.

When Paul urged his listeners to live the Christian life, he wrote, "Let the same mind be in you that was in Christ Jesus" (Phil 2:5). He wanted them to be formed in such a way that they can truly say, "We have the mind of Christ" (1 Cor 2:16b). Putting on the mind of Christ means taking on his way of thinking, his freedom, his approach to life. This is the formation that God wants to create within us through the divine word.

Formational reading of the gospels and other sacred texts shapes us to be like Christ. When we imagine his saving deeds, listen to his teachings, and read about the work of his Holy Spirit in the lives of his followers, we fill our imaginations with the words, images, and vision of life that filled the mind and heart of Jesus. Then, with our minds and hearts engaged, we gradually live more fully in Christ and become formed in his image. Then, filled with hope, we can live in the present world filled with reflections of God's glory while anticipating a future in which all that hides and disfigures God's design is done away with and the glorious presence of God renews the whole creation.

God forms us through scripture by freeing our minds, enlarging our perspectives, and broadening our horizons. In this world today, with all its present ugliness and pain, the Word of God calls us to have the mind of Christ, to embody his gospel, and to be agents of the new creation, when God will bring earth and heaven together, finally and forever. We can live as missionary disciples of Jesus because we know that God's kingdom has broken into our world with Christ's healing and redemption. The formative Word of God enables us to inhabit a world where God reigns, where we can hope with confident trust, and where lost and sinful creatures like ourselves can be transformed into immortal creatures who will live forever in God.

The "God-Breathed" Scriptures

The divinely revealed realities that are presented to us in the texts of scripture have been written under the inspiration of the Holy Spirit. Paul says, "All scripture is inspired by God" (2 Tm 3:16a). In the Greek text, the word is *theo-pneustos*, "God-breathed." God's presence and life have been breathed into sacred scripture. The breath of divine life has been placed in these words. Be assured that Paul's word is *theo-pneustos*, "God-breathed," and not *theo-graptos*, "God-written." God did not write the words of the texts, nor did God dictate the words to human beings. Rather, as in the ancient prophets, "Men and women moved by the Holy Spirit spoke from God" (2 Pt 1:21b).

While God did indeed work within the human authors of scripture, inspiration is not just what God did in the minds and hearts of those biblical writers thousands of years ago. "God-breathed" also describes the Bible today. The sacred texts are always inspired; they are always filled with the Spirit of God. Because scripture is inspired, the voice of God is heard, sounding through the biblical pages and into our hearts. Because of the indwelling Spirit, the word is alive and charged with divine power to change and renew us.

The Holy Spirit, who moved the original authors to write, also works within the prayerful readers of the inspired page. Because of the divine Spirit, the ancient words are also contemporary words. Both the ancient author and the contemporary reader are joined to the living word animated by the Holy Spirit. Although the work of the ancient authors is finished, their writing is forever living because their words are penetrated by the life-giving Spirit.

Through inspiration, scripture is always youthful, offering new insights, challenges, and renewal. The Holy Spirit continues to breathe life and power into the sacred texts, so that on every page we can truly encounter the living Word of God. As Moses experienced God's presence and revelation through the burning bush, we can meet God on the holy ground of the inspired pages of scripture and experience God's presence and divine life within us.

As a living word, not just a collection of literature inherited from past ages, the scriptures captivate us and move us toward God's grace so that we might share in the divine life. Through the Holy Spirit alive in the words of the sacred texts and living in us, the scriptures breathe God's truth, goodness, and beauty. Because these texts are God-breathed, they lead us into a personal, formative encounter with God to the degree that we open our lives to their transforming power.

Experiencing Scripture as Whole Persons

Reading scripture as the Word of God requires that we bring the entirety of our being to the practice. We must respond to God's revelation with our intellect, memory, will, emotions, senses, imagination, drives, and desires. Being transformed by scripture and learning to live "in Christ" is a lifelong process that engages the whole human person.

The ancient spiritual masters encourage us to involve a range of senses in our spiritual practice: seeing, hearing, smelling, tasting, and feeling. For this reason, the ancients always read the scripture aloud: seeing it with their eyes, hearing it with their ears, and pronouncing it with their lips. For this same reason, using icons, candles, incense, chimes, and other sensual stimuli can enhance our experience of the sacred text as the Word of God.

But more than involving the senses, we should strive to read scripture as insiders, as participants in the world of the Bible rather than simply as outsiders looking on from a distance. This means allowing the scenes to become real in our imagination. It means allowing the feelings and emotions expressed in the text to interact with our own. It means acquiring an experiential knowledge of the text rather than simply an intellectual understanding.

This kind of inside reading leads us to respond from within the world of the text. As a participant in the biblical world, we bring our whole self to the reading, with our minds and hearts engaged. The goal of this holistic reading of scripture is an encounter with God.

When we read the gospels, for example, we can come to an intellectual knowledge that God loves us based on the abstract truth that we discover in the text. And although we know with our head that God loves us, sometimes our heart tells us that God just, well, tolerates us. But when we begin reading the narratives of Jesus from the inside, especially scenes in which Jesus encounters suffering, sinful, and struggling people, we allow the truth of God's love to be experienced in our hearts. When we soak in these narratives with our whole self, we can know with our minds and our hearts, feel with our emotions and desires, and truly experience God changing our lives.

Scripture nourishes our embodied spirits as food nourishes our physical bodies. For this reason, we don't just study scripture; we assimilate it. We take it in, eat it, chew it, digest it, and we get those words flowing through our bloodstream. The prophet Ezekiel tells about his vision of God in which the divine being handed him a scroll written on both sides and tells him to eat the scroll:

> He said to me, O mortal, eat what is offered to you; eat this scroll, and go, speak to the house of Israel. So I opened my mouth, and he gave me the scroll to eat. He said to me, Mortal, eat this scroll that I give you and fill your stomach with it. Then I ate it; and in my mouth it was as sweet as honey. He said to me: Mortal, go to the house of Israel and speak my very words to them. (Ez 3:1–4)

God placed his own word into his prophet so that it could become enfleshed in him. God wanted Ezekiel to experience his word with his whole self—his body, mind, heart, will, and spirit—so that he could genuinely proclaim that word to others. Likewise, God wants us to experience scripture deeply so that his word may be digested and nourish our lives. God desires us to assimilate scripture so that it becomes metabolized in works of mercy, healing, and reconciliation. By being digested and metabolized into a form that we may use for God's reign in the world, the sacred text is transformed through us with God's grace into witness and service.

Allowing God's Word to Transform Us

The whole Bible proclaims God's transforming grace. God draws near to us while we are still sinners and delights in us. God yearns for us passionately, inspiring within us a yearning to be in the divine presence and to receive God's healing grace. We don't have to earn or deserve God's transforming power. Rather, it is a divine gift that we must only accept into our lives. We only have to create the necessary conditions within ourselves so that we can receive God's liberating and healing word. These are some of the necessary dispositions for allowing God's word to work deeply within us:

- *Reverence.* When we begin reading scripture, we are entering the mystery of God. God's word is always something more than we can comprehend, and we should never approach it with anything less than veneration and respect. This disposition of reverence before the mystery of God's word instills humility within us. Saint Augustine describes his initial arrogance before God: "Proud as I was, I dared to seek that which only the humble can find." We must accept our profound ignorance with regard to God. Filled with hunger and thirst, yearning and need, we know that we can only listen and receive the divine word. When we reverently open the sacred text, we open our hearts to be formed by God.

- *Openheartedness.* We can receive the grace of God's word when we approach it with a heart open to accept it. There is much within scripture that may confuse, frustrate, and even shock us, possibly causing us to reject it. And there are so many external attractions and internal passions that erect barriers to God's word. We must take away the obstacles and provide the good soil for the seed of God's word to grow within us. But when we free ourselves to be formed by scripture, God gradually opens our hearts and gives us the ability to dedicate ourselves to this divine gift. This purified and opened heart gives us the receptivity that enables us to be progressively transformed by God's word.

- *Expectation.* To receive God's transforming word, we must trust that God is present and speaks to us through the inspired word, and that God desires us and creates a longing for the divine presence within us. This kind of personal trust in a God who cares about us deeply leads us to fully expect to encounter God in the inspired word, to expect God to reveal the divine presence and wisdom as we read. This expectation leads us to read the Bible with empty hands, placing the control in God's hands rather than in our own. Reading with expectation means truly listening, knowing that God's agenda may be different from ours. It means learning how to read the Bible in a way that doesn't require that we have all the answers, but that requires us to stay present to the text as it makes us present to the great mystery of God. It is this trusting expectation that creates the listening ear, the open hands, and the receptive heart that are so necessary to receive God's word in scripture. When we desire God and are ready for God's presence, we will read scripture with expectation, and God's word will invite us into a transforming relationship.

- *Faithfulness*. Transformation through God's word is a gradual process. It takes time, dedication, and persistence for reading sacred texts to saturate our minds, hearts, imaginations, and desires with God's word. The more we get to know God through our reading of scripture, the more we grow in love. Faithfulness to this communication with our divine lover creates an ever-deepening intimacy. And as we come to know God, the better we grow to know and understand ourselves, for we begin to see ourselves through the eyes of God. This faithful practice of reading scripture gradually transforms us into the image of God, into the mind and heart of Christ.

Experiencing God's Word through Icons

J ust as early Christians began writing about the good news of Jesus Christ, they began to express this good news also in images. The same impulse that moved writers to communicate the Gospel with ink on parchment also moved artists to express the Gospel with paint on wood and plaster. And just as the sacred writings began to be read in the Church's liturgy, so the imagery of the Church began to form part of the sacred space for worship in house churches, shrines, and catacombs.

Unfortunately, most of the earliest Christian art has been ruined, either because the instability of the pigments caused them to fade away or because they were destroyed through the persecution of the Church at various times throughout its early history. But just as the original manuscripts of the scriptures were faithfully reproduced by copyists to preserve them, so iconographers preserved sacred images through the centuries by their faithful reproduction of the original forms and symbols of the icons.

There are many ways to be attentive to the mysteries of God's word. One way developed in the ancient Church is by listening to the scriptures; another is by gazing at icons. The inspired texts and the holy icons reproduced in this book invite us to both listen and see deeply. And the purpose of both scripture and icon is to make us present to the saving event. Through both sacred text and sacred image, the grace of the saving event and its transformative power become present and available for us now as we listen and as we gaze.

Both listening and gazing require our complete attention. Saint Benedict, who set the tone for the spirituality of Western Christianity in his *Rule*, urged his followers to "listen" to God's word "with the ear of the heart." The Byzantine writers, however, focused on gazing, i.e., as Paul says, with "the eyes of the heart" (Eph 1:18). Thus, Eastern Christianity emphasizes the visual aspects of encountering the saving mysteries of faith.

Icons are often described as being "written" rather than painted because they are meant to communicate the word of God. The living word, God's self-revelation, is "written" in the biblical texts and in icons. Icons expressing narratives from the life of Jesus and his Church are complimentary to the written gospels. The ninth-century Saint Theodore the Studite links gospel and icon with the senses of hearing and seeing:

> Imprint Christ onto your heart, where he already dwells. Whether you read about him in the gospels or behold him in an icon, may he inspire your thoughts as you come to know him twofold through the twofold experience of your senses. Thus you will see through your eyes what you have learned through the words you have heard. He who in this way hears and sees will fill his entire being with the praise of God. (*Epistolarum Liber*, II.36)

Expressing the Divine in Images

In the Bible, the Greek word *eikon* is usually translated as "image." Genesis tells us that man and woman are made in God's "image" (Gn 1:27), and Paul tells us that Christ is the "image" of the invisible God (Col 1:15). In this sense, you and I are icons, even though sin distorts the image of God in us. Jesus Christ, however, restores this divine image in humanity. He is the living, incarnate icon of God *par excellence*, reflecting perfectly the divine radiance. As we live in him and respond to God's grace, his radiance is revealed in us and we become evermore complete icons.

In this book we are presented with icons of God's saving actions associated with Christ, in whom "the whole fullness of deity dwells bodily" (Col 2:9). These icons express the presence and action of God among us in the saving mysteries and invite us to take part in them. Through the icon, our present world and the world of God's saving history are opened to each other and the grace of salvation is made effective for us now. As we open ourselves to God's transforming graces, we allow God to restore the divine image within us and to make us more like Christ.

Although there is a long and rich tradition of venerating icons in Christianity, there have been periods in which images were forbidden. This ban on images was rooted in the command God gave to Moses, "You shall have no other gods before me. You shall not make for yourself an idol, whether in the form of anything that is in heaven above, or that is on the earth beneath, or that is in the water under the earth" (Ex 20:3–4). In the eighth century, the Christian emperor of the East banned all images and started a smashing campaign, which is called "iconoclasm." Most of the earlier icons were destroyed during this period. Similar iconoclastic tendencies continue today within some divisions of Christianity.

The greatest defender of icons during this period was Saint John of Damascus. In his *Defense Against Those Who Oppose Holy Images*, he begins by expressing the wisdom of the Torah that forbids images of God:

> How wise the Law is! How could one depict the invisible? How picture the inconceivable? How could one express the limitless, the immeasurable, the invisible? How give infinity a shape? How paint immortality? How put mystery in one place?

He then continues his defense of icons by arguing that the worship of false gods is not the same as venerating holy images. It is impossible to make an image of the immeasurable, immortal God, and we should never give true worship to anything but God. However, Christ coming in the flesh as the image of the invisible God changed everything.

> When you think of God, who is a pure spirit, becoming man for your sake, then you can clothe him in a human form. When the invisible becomes visible to the eye, you may then draw his form. When he who is a pure spirit, immeasurable in the boundlessness of his own nature, existing as God, takes on the form of a servant and a body of flesh, then you may draw his likeness and show it to anyone who is willing to contemplate it. Depict his coming down, his virgin birth, his baptism in the Jordan, his Transfiguration on Mt. Tabor, his all-powerful sufferings, his death and miracles, the proofs of his deity, the deeds he performed in the flesh through divine power, his saving Cross, his grave, his resurrection and his ascent into heaven. Give to it all the endurance of engraving and color.

The mystery of the Incarnation is the greatest argument in favor of icons and legitimizes the depiction of the divine. In Christ, God has voluntarily allowed himself to be limited by time and space. The invisible Father has a face in the Son. In Christ, the word of God has become flesh: "The word became flesh and lived among us, and we have seen his glory" (Jn 1:14a); and the image of God has become flesh: "He is the image of the invisible God, the firstborn of all creation" (Col 1:15). Christ is the revealed form of God. About himself, Christ says, "Whoever has seen me has seen the Father" (Jn 14:9).

As a result of the Incarnation, created images are able to carry the divine within themselves. Through Christ's descent into the created world, God participated in human nature, so that we could "become participants in the divine nature" (2 Pt 1:4). The icon bears witness to this mystical interaction between God and creation. The material image is a sacramental sign that mediates the divine presence. The icon points toward the new creation, the redeemed and illuminated creation for which we wait with joyful hope.

Reading Icons

When we read scripture we must emphasize faculties in addition to the intellect because of our cultural overuse of the mind in reading, but when we read icons we must accentuate faculties in addition to the emotions because of our cultural overuse of personal feelings in viewing images. We like art to be pretty, decorative, and undemanding. Our culture blasts us with images constantly, and many of them are designed to appeal to our desires so that we purchase products. But icons are not sweet, promotional, or manipulative. We must read them with the mind as much as with the emotions. And, as with scripture, we must include our heart, imagination, will, and desires.

Icons communicate Christian truth in a visible form. They stand in opposition to theories of modern art in which those who look at a picture are encouraged to make up their own minds about what it means. The truth expressed through an icon is objective and precise. It depicts visually what the Church teaches verbally. It expresses truth that has been passed down through the ages by means of the Church's tradition.

For this reason, iconographers employ traditional motifs and techniques, and the form of particular subjects is depicted very consistently. These have been handed down master to apprentice with remarkably small variation. The artists are not free to incorporate subjective interpretations into the work. The icon does not express an individual spirituality but is designed to express the faith of the Church. The content is determined by sacred scripture and holy tradition.

However, creating an icon is not a process of making an exact copy from a model. Although the painter is bound by tradition and icons of the same subject tend to look very similar, the iconographer enters a process of creative dialogue with a living tradition. Rather than being static, the tradition contains dynamic elements. There is room within the tradition of iconography for further development within certain set limits. This allows for the variations in icons from different historical periods, from diverse regions of the Orthodox world such as variations between Greek and Russian icons, and for differences in the styles of individual artists. Nevertheless, each iconographer is bound more by artistic discipline than by originality.

Icons have been described as theology in line and color. They are the visual language of Eastern Christianity. The Byzantine world in which icons were produced and first viewed was one in which everyone had knowledge of the biblical literature. So icons do not take the place of scripture for the uneducated; rather they are expressions and interpretations of the sacred texts. They are viewed in the context of scripture and its proclamation in the Church's liturgy. Icons express and interpret the Word of God in a way similar to the preaching and writing of the early patristic theologians. So the Byzantine viewer gazing at an icon absorbs the imagery in light of their prior textual knowledge. For this reason, our listening and reflecting on scripture is complemented by our gazing and meditating on sacred images.

The following are some of the characteristics that give icons their unique and sacred quality:

- *Light and color.* Unlike western art in which the light within a scene comes from a particular source and direction, creating angled light and shadow, the light of an icon has no single source. The images within the icon are completely surrounded and infused with light. This suggests that the luminance of an icon comes from "uncreated light," the light of God's kingdom. This light not only permeates the scene but also illumines the viewer standing in prayer before the icon. Likewise, color is affected by this quality of light. The color is applied in layers with tempera, creating a translucent effect in which light seems to penetrate through the color. Choices of color often vary, but gold is always associated with divine splendor and the glory of God's kingdom.

- *Faces and gestures.* The face is a focal point in icons and the eyes of the viewer are drawn there. The face is not designed primarily to be attractive but to express the spiritual qualities that come from within the person. Faces and bodies are frequently elongated and eyes are often unusually large or bright. The direction of the subject's gaze draws the attention of the viewer and a direct gaze with eye contact with the viewer establishes a profound, interpersonal relationship. The gestures, too, direct the scene, and they establish relationships between persons in the icon.

- *Inverse perspective.* The purpose of the icon is not to create the illusion of three-dimensional space; rather, the icon establishes an encounter between the viewer and the image. This effect is created by reversing the perspective from that of a naturalistic scene. In most of western art, the diagonal lines used to create perspective converge into a vanishing point presumably behind the image. These lines create the illusion of depth within the scene. In icons the direction of these lines is reversed, so that the lines converge in front of the image, i.e., at the spectator. This method creates the illusion that the subject of the icon comes to meet the spectator in front of the icon. This inverse perspective intensifies the interpersonal relationship between the subject of the icon and the one gazing at the image.

- *Symbolism.* When iconographers wish to express something that cannot be directly conveyed in images, they turn to symbolism. Since God may not be directly portrayed in an icon, God's presence or intervention is symbolized, often by concentric circles in the heavens, a hand from the clouds, or rays of light from above. Other symbols are expressed with regularity in icons. For example, the Word of God is expressed with a book or scrolls in the hands of the subjects or authors of scripture. A halo radiating from a subject's head symbolizes the person's sanctity and relationship with God. Often, too, the saints are identified by including some symbolic element associated with their lives.

- *Stillness and silence.* The mouths of characters within icons are never open, and there are no images within the scene that indicate sound. In order to identify the persons in the icon, their names are often written next to their image. This silence within the icon creates stillness within the viewer and invites quiet gazing. This meditative quality seems to naturally draw the viewer to prayer and contemplation.

The Practice of Visio Divina

Visio divina is the practice of attentively and receptively gazing upon an image so that the experience leads us to meditation and prayer. While contemplatively looking at the image, we trust that God will illumine our minds and hearts. Although any work of art or natural scene may serve as the image we gaze upon, the icons of Eastern Christianity are particularly suited for this practice. These icons have a sacred subject and a quality of stillness that leads us naturally to a quiet, contemplative experience.

Icons are not made for decoration or museums. Rather, they are created for divine liturgy and for prayerful devotion. The artist begins to create the icon after a period of prayer and fasting. These holy images are set apart for a spiritual purpose. The icon and the area around it become sacred space for prayer. Through the lines and color, the expressions and gestures, and the traditional motifs, the icon leads us into a deepening awareness of the divine presence.

Rather than standing back to objectively observe the scene, the icon becomes the mediator of a personal encounter between ourselves and the subjects depicted in the scene. Through the mediation of the holy icon, we meet Christ and the saints face-to-face. We gaze upon the image expectantly, trusting that the Holy Spirit will use the sacred icon to move our mind and heart. And we anticipate that in some way we will be formed by it.

As with lectio divina, we must create the necessary dispositions within ourselves so that we will be moved and changed through the image. By approaching the icon with reverence and openheartedness, we remove the obstacles that prevent God's grace from working through the image, and we open our hearts to God's transforming presence.

Icons testify to the fact that all creation is sacramental, reflecting the glory of its Creator. In one way or another they all reflect the Incarnation, the entry of the divine into the world of created matter. And for each of us, icons witness to the process of deification, the new creation that God is working within us so that we share in the very nature of God. As we gaze upon them they arouse in us our natural longing for God, reminding us that we are most at home when we are in the presence of God.

The Formative Experience of Lectio and Visio Divina

Inspired scripture and its biblical commentary as well as sacred images and the tradition of iconography developed during the early centuries when the Church was one. In the second millennium, tensions grew between the Latin West and the Greek East, and tragically, in the year 1054, the Great Schism split the Catholic Church and the Orthodox Church. Differences of language and culture as well as political and religious divergences continued to erect barriers between Western and Eastern Christianity.

During the past centuries, Catholicism continued to develop the practice of meditative study of scripture, which we call lectio divina. The practice was preserved through the western monastic tradition beginning with Saint Benedict. Medieval monastic writers described it as a four-step process using the imagery of the ladder, beginning with lectio and climbing to contemplatio. The more active traditions continued to develop the practice. In Dominican spirituality, listening to the word became a preparation for preaching the word. Saint Dominic's eighth way of prayer, sitting with scripture, leads to his ninth way of prayer, walking with scripture. Saint Ignatius of Loyola added dimensions of imagination, consolation, and discernment as he developed the *Spiritual Exercises*. These traditions demonstrate how biblical reflection and prayer leads to both contemplation and witness, forming people into contemplatives in action.

In recent years, lectio divina has been liberated from monasteries and religious houses to become the heart of lay spirituality. Pope Francis recommended lectio divina as a "way of listening to what the Lord wishes to tell us in his word and of letting ourselves be transformed by the Spirit." Lectio divina, he said, "consists of reading God's word in a moment of prayer and allowing it to enlighten and renew us" (*Evangelii Gaudium*, 152).

At the same time that lectio divina developed in Western Christianity, the contemplative gazing on icons continued to flourish in Eastern Christianity. This practice, which many in the West now call *visio divina*, was preserved and refined in the monasteries of the Orthodox Church. Yet, this practice is undertaken by lay people throughout the East, through the liturgy of the Church and also through personal prayer in the home.

Fortunately today, Western Christians are learning to appreciate Eastern iconography and to make use of icons for prayer. Icons are more and more found in Catholic churches and increasingly more Christians are learning to bring icons into their homes and appreciate their beauty and their power to invite contemplation. In educational and retreat experiences, I have taught contemplative practice using a combination of lectio divina and visio divina with fruitful results. Both listening to scripture and gazing on icons can lead to a deep experience of God's living word.

This book combines the practice of lectio divina and visio divina as a way of drawing on the richness of both Western and Eastern spirituality. I have written it with a deep hope in the continual unification of East and West so that the third millennium of Christianity will be marked by a reunification of the Catholic and Orthodox churches. Let us foster that unity by learning to appreciate the traditions of both West and East, so that one day soon the Church will be one, breathing fully with both lungs as the Body of Christ.

Neither East nor West advocates spiritual practices that are rigidly defined, and neither lectio divina nor visio divina require a series of steps to follow. These traditions are better defined as ways of approaching God's living word than any kind of system. However, in order to teach this practice, I have drawn from the tradition to encourage the consecutive focus on six movements: *lectio* (listening), *visio* (gazing), *meditatio* (reflection), *oratio* (prayer), *contemplatio* (contemplation), and *operatio* (witness). So while entering each moment of the practice, realize what is most important. It is not about the correctness of your practice but the inner transformation that you experience.

The following is a brief summary of each of the six movements that will be followed throughout this book:

- *Lectio* is best described as listening deeply to scripture as we read. We savor the words of the sacred literature, appreciating the images, envisioning the scene, feeling the sentiments, and allowing the words to move from our heads to our hearts. We read slowly and carefully, studying the words and characters, the images and metaphors.

  This listening requires that we try to receive God's word with as little prejudgment as possible. In other words, we should read the text as if we were hearing it for the first time. We can't listen fully if we think we already know what the text is going to tell us. Lectio urges us to read expectantly, creating space within us for the new wisdom and understanding that God wants to give us through the sacred page.

  Each biblical text in this book is followed by a brief commentary. This includes some basic insights of biblical scholarship and shows us how to listen to the text with the understanding of the Church. This commentary helps us understand the multiple layers of meaning within the biblical texts and their rich history of interpretation.

When we truly listen to the biblical text in this way, we trust that it is inspired by God and capable of forming us into a fuller image of God.

- *Visio* is gazing upon an image, trusting that God will illumine our minds and hearts through the image. We look at the image not as spectators but as participants in the relationships and holy actions that the image evokes.

    Icons hold a privileged place as vehicles of God's self-revelation through images. Because of their unique qualities, icons awaken in us a holy orientation toward the supernatural. They witness to both the nearness and the otherness of God. When looking at icons, we understand that God is both a loving parent and a God of awesome majesty. They convince us that we can approach God with confidence but never with familiarity. Their quality of stillness calms our souls and invites us to quiet gazing.

    The icons reproduced in this book for visio divina are followed by a brief commentary. Icons express themselves through a holy, symbolic language. While the messages of icons are never overstated, they are also never simple. The commentary includes information about the motifs, forms, characters, and symbols within the icon, and helps the viewer relate the image to the biblical text.

    The icon is a visual gospel. When we truly look at an image in this way, the icon becomes a threshold—a doorway through which we meet the characters in the scene and they come to meet us. We gaze upon the scene with receptive vision, and we allow the encounter provided by the icon to move us deeply.

- *Meditatio* is reflecting on the meaning and message of the sacred text and the sacred image. After listening carefully and gazing attentively, we let the text and image settle within us and penetrate the deepest parts of our being. We let the encounter awaken within us new understandings, questions, and challenges. Our reflection forms connections between the ancient forms of the Gospel and our contemporary lives.

There is a richness of meaning in the Gospel because it is infused with the Spirit of God. We should ask ourselves if there is a particular word or phrase that stands out to us in the text. We should consider what section of the icon draws our attention and stirs our energy. The Gospel has particular messages that can be received by everyone who encounters God's word in the context of daily experiences and in the same Spirit in which it was created.

This book stimulates meditatio through the use of questions. These questions encourage a deeper and more personal consideration of the text and icon. They challenge us to create a kind of dialogue between the inspired word and our life today. By considering each of these questions for reflection, we can facilitate a deeper penetration of the word within us so that it can gradually mold and transform our lives.

- *Oratio* is a verbal and prayerful response to God's word as experienced in the sacred text and icon. If we have truly listened and gazed as God is revealed to us in words and images, we will naturally want to respond to God. In this way, lectio divina and visio divina become a kind of dialogue with God, as we receive God's word and respond to God in prayer.

  Depending on what we have experienced from God in scripture and image, our prayer may be one of praise, thanksgiving, lament, or repentance. And this prayer is increasingly enriched because it is continually nourished by the vocabulary, images, and sentiments of the text and icon. This prayer arises within us as a natural and heartfelt desire to respond to the voice of God whose word we have encountered. This keeps our prayer fresh and personal, preventing it from becoming routine and repetitive.

This book offers us words to begin our prayer. But these prayers presume that we will want to continue praying from our own hearts. Just join the words, ideas, and desires generated through lectio and visio together with the thoughts, needs, and feelings that arise within you. As a Spirit-led response to God, our prayer becomes increasingly intimate and filled with God's grace.

- *Contemplatio* is simply a quiet resting in God. There arrives a time in our verbal prayer when words become unnecessary and no longer helpful. Our spoken response has taken us as far as it can in our relationship with God. Contemplatio is wordless silence in the divine presence. We simply receive the transforming embrace of God who has led us to this moment.

When we feel God drawing us into this deeper awareness of the Holy Spirit, we gradually abandon our intellectual activity and let ourselves be wooed into divine intimacy. We must let go of any effort to be in charge of the process. What God does within us during these moments of stillness is not up to us. We simply accept and receive whatever grace God is offering us.

Sometimes we will want to bring a word or an image from our reflection and prayer into the silence. It can serve as a kind of verbal mantra or visual mandala to maintain our awareness and keep us consciously in God's presence. We can, for example, keep the "eyes of our heart" focused on Mary or Jesus during our contemplation. Imagine them looking with mercy upon us.

All of the material and technological achievements of our day are not without their price. Never before in history have people been more prone to analyze, intellectualize, and control everything about life. And never before has contemplation been more difficult to experience. Because we judge our own life and that of others by successes and achievements and define people primarily by their "doing" rather than their "being," we have suppressed our natural ability for contemplative practice. This has created a void in human life and explains the growing attraction of Eastern spirituality today. We long for a way to relate to God that does not depend on what we accomplish but on who we are at the deepest level.

If we spend all of our time in extroverted activity, we become strangers to our own inner life. By denying ourselves the environment in which to cultivate contemplation, we deny ourselves a fuller understanding of our true self. Lectio divina and visio divina lead us to the experience of contemplatio and to the personal transformation made possible through a deeper relationship with God.

- *Operatio* is faithful living in Christ. Lectio divina and visio divina lead not only to a changed heart but also to a changed life. This practice must make a difference in the way we live. Operatio is the word of God lived out in generous service, in concrete witness, in faithful commitment, and in works of mercy.

As we deepen our relationship with God through the movements of lectio divina and visio divina, our actions become vehicles of God's presence to others. We become "doers of the word, and not merely hearers" (Jas 1:22). We become channels of God's compassion.

Actualization—putting God's word into action—can be as simple as helping a person in need or being kind to someone we don't like. It can be as demanding as a call to reconcile with someone who is estranged from us or an urge to change some aspect of our career. God's word not only communicates ideas, it also contains the power to create change.

Just as the integrity of any person's word is weighted not only by the ideas it contains but also by the results it achieves, so the word of God must achieve its purposes. God speaks in the words of Isaiah: "So shall my word be that goes out from my mouth; it shall not return to me empty, but it shall accomplish that which I purpose, and succeed in the thing for which I sent it" (Is 55:11). Lectio divina and visio divina shape our being and thereby shape our action. From this process of personal growth and renewal flows the witness of Christian discipleship.

The Annunciation

Lectio

Be still in mind and body as you prepare to experience the inspired Word. Light a candle, ring a bell or chime, kiss the text, or perform some other action to help you focus on the sacred text. Breathe slowly, calling on the same Holy Spirit who filled the sacred writers to fill your heart. Read the text aloud, seeing the text with your eyes, vocalizing the text with your lips, and hearing the text with your ears.

Luke 1:26–38

In the sixth month the angel Gabriel was sent by God to a town in Galilee called Nazareth, to a virgin engaged to a man whose name was Joseph, of the house of David. The virgin's name was Mary. And he came to her and said, "Greetings, favored one! The Lord is with you." But she was much perplexed by his words and pondered what sort of greeting this might be. The angel said to her, "Do not be afraid, Mary, for you have found favor with God. And now, you will conceive in your womb and bear a son, and you will name him Jesus. He will be great, and will be called the Son of the Most High, and the Lord God will give to him the throne of his ancestor David. He will reign over the house of Jacob forever, and of his kingdom there will be no end." Mary said to the angel, "How can this be, since I am a virgin?" The angel said to her, "The Holy Spirit will come upon you, and the power of the Most High will overshadow you; therefore the child to be born will be holy; he will be called Son of God. And now, your relative Elizabeth in her old age has also conceived a son; and this is the sixth month for her who was said to be barren. For nothing will be impossible with God." Then Mary said, "Here am I, the servant of the Lord; let it be with me according to your word." Then the angel departed from her.

God's intervention in the world through Mary was unlike anything ever before in the history of salvation. Although God had prepared the way through the deeds of other remarkable women of Israel, Mary's virginal conception highlights the radical newness of God's action. God's unexpected grace was not a response to her yearning for a child, nor was it the result of anything she could have anticipated. God was doing an extraordinarily new thing in response to the watchful longing of God's people. The child to be born would be the Messiah, the One who would be given the throne of David with an unending kingdom, and he would be the Son of God because he would be conceived through the overshadowing power of God's Spirit.

Mary was among the most powerless in her society. She was poor in a culture in which wealth was esteemed; she was female in a world in which men ruled; she was young in a society in which age was honored. That she should be highly favored by God shows how God works—continually reversing the expectations of the world and lifting up the lowly.

Mary's son would be a divine king. Unlike David, whose reign was bounded by the borders of time and Israel's empire, this king would fulfill all of history and embrace all of time, and "of his kingdom there will be no end." But he would not come from splendid palaces, arrayed in royal robes, and doing battle with enemies. He would come through Mary's womb, a hungry and crying child, the hope of the entire world.

At the annunciation, Luke begins to portray Mary as the original model of the Christian believer and disciple. Although she is favored with God's grace, she does not understand. She asks, "How can this be?" and the angel replies, "The Holy Spirit will come upon you, and the power of the Most High will overshadow you." Without comprehending God's plan, she accepts her mission with trust: "Here am I, the servant of the Lord; let it be with me according to your word." Mary opens a space for the divine presence to dwell within her, enabling God to make a new home within all of humankind. Saint Augustine said that Mary, full of faith, conceived Christ first in her heart before conceiving him in her womb.

Visio

Gaze upon this image and let it draw you into the scene.
Fix your eyes upon the face and gestures of both the angel
and Mary. Imagine the emotions present in this scene,
and let them lead you into the heart of Mary. Notice the
colors and symbols and seek to relate them to the biblical
text. Let the uncreated light of the icon illumine your
heart with God's grace.

The annunciation is an event that must be approached with quiet and deep reverence. It is the mystery by which Christ entered the world. In Mary, heaven and earth meet. The divide that separated God and humanity begins to be healed. For this reason, the icon of the annunciation is often placed on the royal doors of Orthodox churches, the gateway to the sanctuary. This mystery of the Word incarnate in the Virgin Mary leads worshipers into the holy and saving presence of God. Just as Mary received Christ—body, blood, soul, and divinity—at the annunciation, we experience the same in the holy Eucharist.

Gabriel is one of God's archangels. The wings symbolize his work as a divine messenger, able to serve God with quick and agile service. The bright robes radiate with divine energy and suggest an ethereal existence, and the angel's feet suggest that he is hovering above the ground. The greeting of the angel—"Shalom Miriam, Ave Maria, Hail Mary"—has been the source for some of the world's most beautiful music and the inspiration for some of the world's finest art.

Mary has risen from her seat, ready to listen. Her right hand is turned upward, suggesting her initial reserve—"How can this be?"—but her bowed head prepares for her humble submission to God's will. She has been given the honored title of *Theotokos*—the one who gives birth to the One who is God.

In the tradition of ancient Israel, the mother of the king in the line of David received great honor. Sitting on a throne to the right of her son, she was considered the queen in the kingdom and an advocate for the people (1 Kgs 2:19–20). As the fulfillment of this tradition, Mary will be the royal mother in the kingdom of her Son, and her seat and the cushions behind her suggest a throne. The humble maiden will become the queen of heaven and earth.

Mary holds a spindle of scarlet yarn, which will become a veil for the Temple sanctuary. Although this veil concealed the holy of holies, the place of God's mysterious presence, the child beginning to form within her womb will be the new temple and reveal the fullness of God. Christ himself as the Son of God is shown in the divine realm at the top of the icon, the One who will be formed in Mary's womb as she freely and selflessly says "yes" to the word of God.

Meditatio

Reflect on the inspired text and sacred icon so that God's word becomes a living word for you. Allow the text and image to interact with your own world of memories, concerns, and hopes until you become aware of the personal messages the divine word is offering to you today.

- Gabriel's salutation, "Greetings, favored one!"—literally, "Rejoice, you who have been filled with grace!"—indicates that the angel knows more about Mary than she realized about herself. The divine grace working within her was a gift of God's love. Ponder these words as Mary did, and let them lead you to an awareness of God's desire for you.

- The message of the angel to Mary reveals the identity of Jesus and some of his most important titles. What do these words suggest to you about the nature of Mary's Son and the type of mission he will receive?

- God worked in the life of Mary, not because of her own merits or worthiness, but because of her trusting faith. How does the annunciation show how God works in the lives of his people? What hope does this offer to you?

- Fear and insecurities so often enslave people and close them off from life's possibilities. Gabriel's urging Mary not to fear and Mary's calm acceptance illustrate a way to overcome anxiety in order to live with more freedom. In what ways do you desire to live more fully? How can this meditation help you to do that?

- Mary received the word of God in her heart and thus consented to conceive the Son of God in her womb. How can the example of Mary teach you how to receive God's word and allow it to transform your life?

- What feelings might Mary have experienced at the message of the angel? What might have been most difficult for her? How can her acceptance give you courage? When do you need to hear the words of the angel: "Nothing will be impossible with God"?

Oratio

Respond in prayer to God's word to you, imitating the trusting faith and humble acceptance of Mary. Begin with this prayer, then continue to pray in your own words.

- Most High God, who surprised and blessed Mary with the revelation of your plan for her life, show me how to receive your grace with trust and humility. Teach me how to prepare my heart to truly hear your voice as you speak your word to me, so that your will may be done in me. May I turn to Mary, your favored daughter, so that I can receive your word and that it might take flesh in my life. . . .

Contemplatio

When the words of your prayer begin to seem inadequate and no longer necessary, move into wordless contemplative prayer.

- Ask that the power of the Holy Spirit overshadow you as you rest in God's presence. With a receptive heart like Mary, simply receive the grace God wishes to give you at this moment.

Operatio

Consider ways that you would like to act on your experience of God's word today, and make a commitment to change one aspect of your life.

- Awareness of God's presence and receptivity to God's will gradually transform human life, releasing fears and relieving anxiety. In what ways do you desire to live more fully and freely as a result of your prayerful reflection on the annunciation? How will you accomplish this today?

The
Visitation

Lectio

Pregnancy is filled with anticipation. As you listen to this text, which focuses on two pregnant women, try to create a feeling of expectancy within yourself. Anticipate the transforming power that the Word of God offers for your life. Let yourself experience the joy that fills the sacred page as Mary and Elizabeth meet each other with the hope of God's people in their wombs.

Luke 1:39–49, 56

In those days Mary set out and went with haste to a Judean town in the hill country, where she entered the house of Zechariah and greeted Elizabeth. When Elizabeth heard Mary's greeting, the child leaped in her womb. And Elizabeth was filled with the Holy Spirit and exclaimed with a loud cry, "Blessed are you among women, and blessed is the fruit of your womb. And why has this happened to me, that the mother of my Lord comes to me? For as soon as I heard the sound of your greeting, the child in my womb leaped for joy. And blessed is she who believed that there would be a fulfillment of what was spoken to her by the Lord."

And Mary said,

> "My soul magnifies the Lord,
>   and my spirit rejoices in God my Savior,
> for he has looked with favor on the lowliness of his
>   servant.
>   Surely, from now on all generations will call me
>   blessed;
> for the Mighty One has done great things for me,
>   and holy is his name. . . ."

And Mary remained with her about three months and then returned to her home.

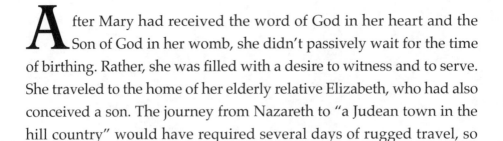

After Mary had received the word of God in her heart and the Son of God in her womb, she didn't passively wait for the time of birthing. Rather, she was filled with a desire to witness and to serve. She traveled to the home of her elderly relative Elizabeth, who had also conceived a son. The journey from Nazareth to "a Judean town in the hill country" would have required several days of rugged travel, so great was Mary's yearning to share the good news and to come to the aid of her elder.

Both women lived in simple villages, Mary in Galilee and Elizabeth in Judea. One is young and full of eagerness about the future; the other is old and wise with the experience of the past. Both are deeply imbued with the scriptures and the tradition of their Jewish faith. Elizabeth is the wise mentor, who offers her young relative the strength of experience. Mary is the generous novice, desiring to help Elizabeth cope with a difficult pregnancy. In these two strong women, bearing their tiny yet-to-be-born children, the dawn of salvation is about to unfold.

With prophetic insight, Elizabeth proclaims that Mary is uniquely blessed by God. First, she is blessed as the mother of Jesus: "Blessed are you among women, and blessed is the fruit of your womb." And second, Mary is blessed as the model disciple: "Blessed is she who believed that there would be a fulfillment of what was spoken to her by the Lord." As both mother and disciple, Mary is the ideal woman of the word of God.

The Canticle of Mary overflows from her joyful and grateful heart. Her song becomes the climax of a long line of songs of praise sung by women in the scriptures of Israel: Miriam (Ex 15:20–21), Deborah (Jgs 5), Hannah (1 Sm 2:1–10), and Judith (Jdt 16:1–17). Mary sings back to God the truths that she has learned in her daily reflection on the Word of God in light of what God is now doing in her life. Her canticle rings with pure praise of God, calling him lord, savior, mighty, and holy. Mary remains always a model of living faith because she recognized what God was doing through her, she accepted it joyfully, and she was humble enough to give God all the glory.

Visio

Gaze upon this image and let it draw you into an encoun-
ter with the four figures in the scene. Notice the faces and
gestures of each person. Consider the relationship of the
figures to the words of the biblical text. Let the embrace
and the emotions expressed here move your heart with
admiration for God's saving plan.

The icon captures the moment of embrace. Mary "set out and went with haste" to see Elizabeth, and now her journey has reached its destination. Their flowing mantles lead us to assume that they ran with eager anticipation to one another. Rejoicing in the pregnancy of the other and in God's power made manifest in their lives, they must have fallen into each other's arms, embracing and dancing with joy.

Elizabeth, who is from the ancient line of Aaron, along with her husband, Zechariah, who is a priest of the Temple in Jerusalem, represents the best in ancient Israel. Like Sarah and many other women of old, Elizabeth is elderly and previously unable to bear a child. She will give birth to a son, John the Baptist, who will be the last great figure of the age of Israel.

Mary is also a woman of Israel, yet she lives in faraway Galilee. Unlike Elizabeth, Mary is a young virgin, representing the newness of God's plans for the world. She will give birth to a son, Jesus, who will bring the new age of salvation to the whole earth. Mary is a model of evangelization who, having experienced good news, is eager to share it with joy. She not only hears the word of God, but she also ponders it and witnesses to it and thus becomes an active contemplative.

In this scene, the old covenant and the new covenant meet and embrace. In Mary, the new covenant reaches out to the old, affirming its crucial significance in God's plan and preparing for its culmination. In Elizabeth, the old covenant recognizes its own fulfillment and honors the coming of the new. They find in each other an instant alliance. Their joyful unity expresses the harmony between the traditional faith of Israel and the coming of the Savior, a completion and new beginning of God's saving work in the world.

As the Ark of the Covenant manifested the presence of the Lord among the people of ancient Israel, Mary is the new bearer of God's presence in the world. King David was filled with awe before the ark of the Lord; Elizabeth is filled with the Holy Spirit and amazed that the mother of the Lord should come to her. As the Ark of the Covenant was greeted with acclamations of joy, leaping, and dancing by the people of Israel, so Elizabeth rejoiced and "the child leaped in her womb."

Meditatio

Spend some time reflecting on the inspired text and sacred icon. Let the questions and insights arise within you as you personally encounter the auditory and the visible word of God and allow it to interact with your own life today.

- Mary "set out and went with haste" to the house of Zechariah and Elizabeth. When have you gone with haste to share good news with another? Compare your emotions with those that Mary must have felt.

- Mary is the representative and embodiment of the Church, the People of God. What is the connection between what God has done for her and what God wants to accomplish in your own life? How can Mary be a model and mentor for you?

- God's timing is difficult for both Elizabeth and Mary. It would have been easier if Elizabeth had given birth to her son at an earlier age. It would have been easier if Mary had conceived her child after her marriage to Joseph. How do these women help you accept the many difficulties that come with saying yes to God?

- This icon shows Mary as a very young woman, probably in mid-adolescence, Elizabeth as elderly, and John and Jesus as unborn children. What is your usual response to adolescents, the elderly, and the unborn? God shows us how salvation flows through these various stages of life. What can you do to honor the young, the old, and the powerless?

- The ancient Church named Mary as the new Ark of the Covenant and as the *Theotokos*, the bearer of the One who is God. In what ways does the icon express these mysteries in the image of Mary?

- Mary is the ideal woman of God's word. After hearing the word of God, she hastens to share that word with another in need. She surrenders herself to God's plan, she is full of gratitude for the gifts she receives, and she has a contemplative sense of wonder at the mysteries of God. What qualities of Mary do you want to imitate in order to become a person of God's word?

Oratio

After listening and gazing on this mystery of faith, respond from your heart to what you have heard and seen. As Mary prayed her canticle, let your words sound from your lips in praise of God.

- Mighty and Holy One, who has looked upon Mary with favor, grace, and blessings, and has promised the same for the whole world, open my heart to receive your redeeming love. Teach me to wait in joyful expectation for the fulfillment of your saving promises. . . .

Contemplatio

Let yourself rest in God's presence, free from the necessity of words or images. Simply accept the grace God wishes to give you in this moment.

- Let God's presence surround and embrace you and fill you with a love like that of Mary. Consider the love that Mary has for her divine Son and be grateful for her maternal love.

Operatio

Determine ways to respond in action to your experience of God's word, and decide how you will actualize God's word today.

- Elizabeth and Mary enriched the lives of one another because they responded to God's word, rejoiced in God's goodness, and encouraged each other to receive God's grace each day. What would happen if you shared faith and joy more intimately with a trusted relative or friend?

The Nativity of Christ

Lectio

Involve as many of your physical senses as possible as you prepare to read aloud the sacred page. Use scented oil or a fragrant candle to help you create a holy space for your encounter with the Word of God. Let your physical senses open your spiritual senses to God's transforming presence.

Luke 2:7–19

[Mary] gave birth to her firstborn son and wrapped him in bands of cloth, and laid him in a manger, because there was no place for them in the inn.

In that region there were shepherds living in the fields, keeping watch over their flock by night. Then an angel of the Lord stood before them, and the glory of the Lord shone around them, and they were terrified. But the angel said to them, "Do not be afraid; for see—I am bringing you good news of great joy for all the people: to you is born this day in the city of David a Savior, who is the Messiah, the Lord. This will be a sign for you: you will find a child wrapped in bands of cloth and lying in a manger." And suddenly there was with the angel a multitude of the heavenly host, praising God and saying,

> "Glory to God in the highest heaven,
> and on earth peace among those whom he favors!"

When the angels had left them and gone into heaven, the shepherds said to one another, "Let us go now to Bethlehem and see this thing that has taken place, which the Lord has made known to us." So they went with haste and found Mary and Joseph, and the child lying in the manger. When they saw this, they made known what had been told them about this child; and all who heard it were amazed at what the shepherds told them. But Mary treasured all these words and pondered them in her heart.

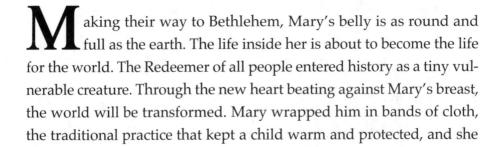

Making their way to Bethlehem, Mary's belly is as round and full as the earth. The life inside her is about to become the life for the world. The Redeemer of all people entered history as a tiny vulnerable creature. Through the new heart beating against Mary's breast, the world will be transformed. Mary wrapped him in bands of cloth, the traditional practice that kept a child warm and protected, and she laid him in a manger, a trough for feeding animals. He who will feed the whole world with the good news of salvation now lies in a manger because there is no place for him to lodge.

But for now, only the shabby shepherds learn the significance of this birth. They are stunned by divine glory and struck with fear. Yet to them, the angel of God proclaims "good news of great joy for all the people," tidings that will be sung down through the ages in gratitude for this night. In explaining that the child born in David's city is Savior, Messiah, and Lord, the angel sums up the whole message of the Gospel. As Savior, Jesus will rescue humanity from sin and heal the divisions that separate people from God and one another. As Messiah, Jesus is the anointed heir of David, the One who will establish God's kingdom. As Lord, Jesus is proclaimed as transcendent and divine.

The "sign" given by the angels, a baby wrapped in cloth and lying in a feeding trough, is not the kind of iconic figure one might expect at the birth of the Savior, Messiah, and Lord. The simplicity of the sign contrasts with the child's proclaimed identity. Both his poverty and his sovereignty invite us to ponder the mystery of this humble Redeemer who will call the weak and lowly to himself.

The angel is joined by a throng of the heavenly chorus praising God at the announcement of Christ's birth. This canticle of angels, the song of glory, became a refrain sung by the early disciples in Christian worship. It proclaims that heaven has touched earth in this wondrous birth. The angels give glory to God who reigns in heaven, and they evoke peace for the people of the earth. This harmony of heaven and earth is the peace that Jesus Christ brings to the world.

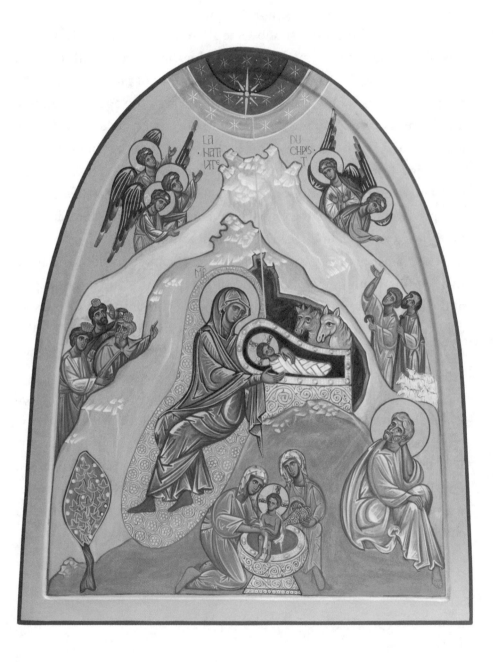

Visio

Consider this icon as the multifaceted image that Mary carried in her heart as she remembered the birth of her divine child. Notice the symbols and gestures as they are illumined by the golden light of the icon. As you let the image draw you into the scene, take time to ponder this union of heaven and earth.

A t the center of the scene is the mother and child. With one hand Mary caresses her child; with the other, she invites all to come and see the sign: "You will find a child wrapped in bands of cloth and lying in a manger." This "sign" not only highlights the meaning of Jesus's life at its beginning, but it also points to his life's end. The One who is born in a stable with animals will die on a cross with criminals. The child "wrapped in bands of cloth and lying in a manger" (Lk 2:12) anticipates the crucified One who will be "wrapped in a linen cloth and laid in a rock-hewn tomb" (Lk 23:53).

This manger is highlighted by the evangelists because it evokes the words of the prophet Isaiah: "The ox knows its owner, and the donkey its master's crib; but Israel does not know, my people do not understand" (Is 1:3). This ancient prophecy is the reason iconographers introduced the donkey and the ox into the Nativity icon. The image suggests that God's people have begun to know their Master's manger, as the shepherd and the Magi find their Lord's manger and glorify God.

In the Gospel of Luke, the Nativity of Christ is manifested by an angel to the shepherds; in the Gospel of Matthew, it is manifested by a star to the Magi. The shepherds with their sheep are seen on the right of the icon. They are the lowly of the land, holding no social or religious status. The Magi, on the left of the icon, are wise men from the East. Both shepherds and Magi come to Bethlehem; they see the child and believe. They represent the people to whom the Lord's coming will be manifested throughout the gospels—the lowly outcasts of the land of Israel and the Gentiles from foreign nations.

The child is fully divine and fully human. Above the mother and child the heavens proclaim the birth, while below them two nursemaids wash the newborn, as is done at every birth on earth. At the corner of the icon is Joseph, perplexed by all the contradictions involved with this birth and struggling with disbelief. Mary looks at him with her inviting gesture, and he becomes the protector of Mary and adoptive father of his divine Son.

Meditatio

The gospel says that Mary treasured all these words and pondered them in her heart. She did not completely understand as yet, but she received these mysteries into the depth of her being. Let the gospel and the icon invite you into this treasure of imagery to impress upon your heart.

- The "sign" given by the angel to the shepherds is the child wrapped in bands of cloth and lying in a manger. Ponder this visible sign of a spiritual reality. What are these bands of cloth? Is the child lying in a manger for feeding, in a darkened tomb, or on an altar as the bread of life?

- According to the ancient prophecy of Isaiah, the ox and ass put us humans to shame (Is 1:3). Isaiah also said, "The wolf shall live with the lamb, the leopard shall lie down with the kid, the calf and the lion and the fatling together, and a little child shall lead them" (Is 11:6). How can the lesser creatures of the earth lead you to recognize and better understand God's ways?

- Which figure in the icon can best lead you to seek and find Christ? The star, the angels, the Magi, the shepherds, the animals? They all point the way for us, so follow in the way that seems best to you.

- Mary is the humble maiden who bore the One who is God; she wrapped in swaddling clothes the One who holds all creation; she fed at her breasts the One who is the food of life. What is Mary teaching you and inviting you to in this scene?

- Because Christ did not choose wealth and power, we can come to him in rags and tags and not be embarrassed. In the fourth century, Saint Athanasius wrote, "He became what we are that we might become what he is." What hope does this teaching offer to you?

- Paul says of Jesus, "He was rich, yet for your sakes he became poor, so that by his poverty you might become rich" (2 Cor 8:9). How does the poverty and weakness of Christ provide you with abundance and strength?

Oratio

Mary is the offering of our humanity as the instrument of the Incarnation and she is humanity's perfect response to God's gift. Begin your prayer with this traditional Orthodox hymn of the Nativity, then continue with your own heartfelt words.

- What shall we offer you, O Christ, who for our sakes has appeared on earth as man? Every creature made by you offers you thanks: the angels offer a hymn; the heavens, a star; the Magi, gifts; the shepherds, their wonder; the earth, its cave; the wilderness, a manger. And we offer you a virgin mother. O pre-eternal God, have mercy on us. . . .

Contemplatio

During the Christmas season, Orthodox Christians greet one another with the words, "Christ is born!" and respond, "Glorify him!" As the words of your prayer begin to seem inadequate, use these words as a contemplative mantra.

- Repeat slowly and continually, "Christ is born!" "Glorify him!"

Operatio

Choose a way that you wish to act on this experience of God's audible and visible word today.

- Consider the figure of Joseph in the icon, and decide how you will move from doubt and bewilderment to a richer experience of life. Let Mary and her Son invite you into a fuller and more active faith.

The Presentation
in the Temple

Lectio

Imagine approaching the Temple in Jerusalem with Jesus, Mary, and Joseph. Call upon the renewing Spirit of God as you prepare to read the gospel, opening yourself to whatever new insights or encouragement God wishes to offer you.

Luke 2:22–35

When the time came for their purification according to the law of Moses, they brought him up to Jerusalem to present him to the Lord (as it is written in the law of the Lord, "Every firstborn male shall be designated as holy to the Lord"), and they offered a sacrifice according to what is stated in the law of the Lord, "a pair of turtledoves or two young pigeons."

Now there was a man in Jerusalem whose name was Simeon; this man was righteous and devout, looking forward to the consolation of Israel, and the Holy Spirit rested on him. It had been revealed to him by the Holy Spirit that he would not see death before he had seen the Lord's messiah. Guided by the Spirit, Simeon came into the Temple; and when the parents brought in the child Jesus, to do for him what was customary under the law, Simeon took him in his arms and praised God, saying,

> "Master, now you are dismissing your servant in peace,
>   according to your word;
> for my eyes have seen your salvation,
> which you have prepared in the presence of all peoples,
> a light for revelation to the Gentiles
>   and for glory to your people Israel."

And the child's father and mother were amazed at what was being said about him. Then Simeon blessed them and said to his mother Mary, "This child is destined for the falling and the rising of many in Israel, and to be a sign that will be opposed so that the inner thoughts of many will be revealed—and a sword will pierce your own soul too."

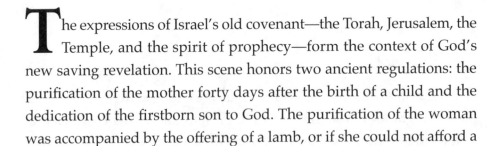

The expressions of Israel's old covenant—the Torah, Jerusalem, the Temple, and the spirit of prophecy—form the context of God's new saving revelation. This scene honors two ancient regulations: the purification of the mother forty days after the birth of a child and the dedication of the firstborn son to God. The purification of the woman was accompanied by the offering of a lamb, or if she could not afford a lamb, she could bring two pigeons or turtledoves. The dedication of the firstborn fulfills the ancient law that the one born first belongs to God, who saved Israel's firstborn on the night of Passover. This dedication of Jesus indicates his lifelong consecration to God's service.

Simeon personifies ancient Israel, his life rooted in tradition and filled with expectant hope. In this elderly man Israel acknowledges the end of a long wait and the beginning of a new age of salvation. The old Israel can rest in peace as the new, messianic age of Israel arises. Simeon's awaiting "the consolation of Israel" refers to the age spoken about by the prophet Isaiah when Israel will be comforted and God's glory will be revealed to all people (Is 40).

The Holy Spirit had revealed to Simeon that he would not die until he had seen God's messiah. As he takes the six-week-old Son of Mary in his arms, he praises God for keeping his word. Now at this turning point in history, he could be dismissed as he welcomes the salvation of all peoples. Simeon's proclamation of the universal significance of Christ's salvation amazes Mary and Joseph and anticipates the entire ministry of Jesus and his Church.

Yet, in the midst of this narrative so filled with light, joy, and hope, Simeon speaks foreboding words directly to Mary. He reveals that God's salvation will not be accomplished without great cost. Jesus is destined to be "a sign that will be opposed." The sign of the Nativity, the infant wrapped in cloths and lying in a manger, will lead to the sign of Jesus crucified and buried. He will evoke a divided response: spurned and rejected by some, received and accepted by others. And, almost as a whisper, he tells Mary that she will share intimately in the pain and rejection that her Son will experience: "a sword will pierce your own soul too."

Visio

Gaze into the faces of these holy ones and let their ges-
tures lead you into a participation in the scene. Imagine
the chanting of Simeon's canticle and the mixture of feel-
ings in the heart of each person. Let the golden light of
the Temple invite you into God's realm to be blessed by
the incarnate Savior.

Here in the Temple of Jerusalem, Mary has just given her Son into the arms of Simeon. Recognizing the child as the long-awaited Messiah of Israel, he shows deep reverence, bowing low and holding Christ with covered hands. Rather than a helpless babe-in-arms, the Lord and Savior blesses those present with the traditional gesture of Orthodox Christianity.

The figure on the left is Joseph, the husband of Mary and adoptive father of Jesus. He holds the two doves that they have brought to the Temple, one for a burnt offering and the other for a sin offering, as stipulated by the Torah (Lv 12:8). Despite the perplexing doubts he exhibits in the Nativity icon, here Joseph is reconciled to Mary and trusts that the infant is truly the Messiah.

The figure between Joseph and Mary is Anna, holding a scroll of prophecy. She is described in the gospel as a "prophet," making her the last of a line of women prophets in Israel, including Miriam, Deborah, and Huldah. Anna is eighty-four years old and has experienced three stages of life: as a single woman, as a married woman for seven years, and as a widow for the many years that followed (Lk 2:36–38). Her constant prayer and fasting have given her insights into the mystery of the child before her. She praised God and spoke about the child and the redemption God would bring her people through him. With Simeon, she represents Israel's longing for the fulfillment of God's promises. Together they stand at the juncture where the old covenant meets the new, and they are able to glimpse before their death the new age of salvation that God is bringing through Jesus.

This scene of Jesus's presentation takes place in the Temple of Jerusalem, but the features have taken on the characteristics of an Orthodox Christian Church. The gates of the Temple resemble the royal doors, the central doors of the iconostasis that open into the sanctuary. The four-pillared dome is a *kivorion*, a canopy in the sanctuary representing the realm of God. Jesus himself is presented as the One who will be the sacrificial offering of the new covenant.

Of course, Jesus did not need to be dedicated to God nor did any sacrifice need to be offered. Jesus enters the Temple not to be purified but to purify Simeon, Anna, and the whole system of Jewish sacrifice with his own offering of a pure and contrite heart.

Meditatio

After listening carefully to the gospel text and gazing with wonder on the icon, consider the personal messages and challenges offered to you by God's revelation. Let these words and images interact with your own experiences of faith and family.

- The Presentation of Jesus shows that God's new work is the fulfillment of ancient promises. Memory is always the foundation of future hope. In what ways is this true in the Bible and in your own life?

- Simeon and Anna have been waiting many years for the day that Jesus would come to the Temple. What do these two figures of Israel teach you about the value of watchful waiting? What promises are you waiting to be fulfilled?

- Have you ever seen advantages of relying on God's timetable instead of your own? Why is patient expectation the necessary stance of every believer?

- Simeon's prophecy to Mary, "a sword will pierce your own soul too," foretells the price that Mary will pay for her intimate love of her Son. How might Mary have felt when Simeon addressed this prophecy to her? What are some of the ways in which the heart of Mary will be pierced throughout the life of Jesus?

- Our Lady of Sorrows shows us that grace is almost always accompanied by grief. While a life of affliction can certainly be a terrible heartbreak, the wounds of suffering can be the instruments for enlarging the human heart. What does Mary teach you about suffering?

- Have you ever had the opportunity to change your view of suffering from senseless tragedy to an opportunity for grace to enter your life? How can Mary teach you to suffer in ways that expand your heart and that help others see meaning and hope in the midst of pain?

Oratio

Respond to God's word to you with your own prayer from the heart. Include ideas, images, and vocabulary from scripture to enrich the content of your prayer. Start with this prayer, then add your own words.

- Lord God, who has brought salvation to the world through your Son, let me receive Jesus into my arms and let his love penetrate my heart. Give me the gift of faith so that I may trust in you completely, the gift of hope that I may see past life's suffering, and the gift of love that I may savor your presence. . . .

Contemplatio

When the words become too many or inadequate, rest with God in wordless contemplative prayer.

- Simeon and Anna had waited a lifetime for the coming of Jesus Christ to them. Try to imagine the experience of holding someone you've waited for your whole life. Spend time in contemplating the gift of Jesus Christ who has come into your heart.

Operatio

Decide how you can actualize the transforming experience of God's word today. Choose a way you wish to change your thinking, feeling, and behavior after this encounter.

- Each of the figures in the icon of the Presentation is exemplary for his or her trust in God. Consider which of these you want to imitate today and seek to be formed by that desire. How could your life be different if you trusted God completely?

Jesus Is Found in the Temple

Lectio

Quiet your external and internal distractions, dedicating this time for sacred conversation with God. Use your imagination to place yourself in this scene. Consider the experiences of your five physical senses and the variety of emotions that pervade the narrative. Let them lead you to a deeper encounter with God's Word.

Luke 2:41–52

Now every year his parents went to Jerusalem for the festival of the Passover. And when he was twelve years old, they went up as usual for the festival. When the festival was ended and they started to return, the boy Jesus stayed behind in Jerusalem, but his parents did not know it. Assuming that he was in the group of travelers, they went a day's journey. Then they started to look for him among their relatives and friends. When they did not find him, they returned to Jerusalem to search for him. After three days they found him in the Temple, sitting among the teachers, listening to them and asking them questions. And all who heard him were amazed at his understanding and his answers. When his parents saw him they were astonished; and his mother said to him, "Child, why have you treated us like this? Look, your father and I have been searching for you in great anxiety." He said to them, "Why were you searching for me? Did you not know that I must be in my Father's house?" But they did not understand what he said to them. Then he went down with them and came to Nazareth, and was obedient to them. His mother treasured all these things in her heart.

And Jesus increased in wisdom and in years, and in divine and human favor.

⊙

This narrative is the only account of Jesus's adolescence in the gospels. It is transitional in the story of Jesus's life, creating a less abrupt movement from his infancy to adulthood. As a revelation of Jesus's identity, it stands between the revelations about Jesus by others during the conception and birth accounts and the revelations that Jesus himself will proclaim throughout his public ministry.

Pilgrims to Jerusalem traveled together for company and for safety. Joseph, Mary, and Jesus traveled in a caravan along with their relatives and neighbors from the village of Nazareth. The twelve-year-old Jesus, expected to be traveling with his extended family, went missing. The frantic search that followed and the reprimand of Jesus by his mother are expected responses to the loss of a child in a large city.

The scene forms the occasion for the first of only two conversations we hear between Jesus and Mary in the gospels. Like any mother would, Mary scolds Jesus: "Child, why have you treated us like this? Look, your father and I have been searching for you in great anxiety." The response of Jesus would provide little consolation for any parent: "Did you not know that I must be in my Father's house?" Jesus's answer makes it clear that his life involves obedience to more than his earthly parents. Although Mary has just referred to Joseph as Jesus's father, Jesus uses the word "Father" to refer to the God of Israel. His answer indicates a deep sense of identity and understanding of his life's purpose.

The loss of the child Jesus and his finding "after three days" antici-pates the adult life of Jesus and his final pilgrimage to Jerusalem for the feast of Passover. Again Jesus will enter the Temple and amaze many with his understanding and his answers. Jesus was never truly lost; instead, he was in the place he most belonged. His ultimate destiny was being with the Father. In his final journey to Jerusalem, Jesus will again be separated from his mother. Again she will feel the pains of not fully understanding the tragic suffering of her son, yet she will trust that Jesus must be about the work of his Father. And just as Mary found Jesus after three days as a child in Jerusalem, she will find him again after three days when he is raised by the Father to new life.

Visio

Let the icon draw you into a spiritual experience of this gospel narrative. Gaze first upon the figure of Jesus, noticing his halo, vestments, and gestures. Then fix your eyes on each of the other figures that surround him. Let the uncreated light of the icon illumine your heart with God's grace.

For all faithful Jews, the Temple was the focus of God's presence in the world and the center of their worship. Seated in the Temple, Jesus is shown to embody Israel's sacred tradition. At the age of twelve, he was considered by Jewish custom as ready to accept the responsibilities of the Torah and its imperatives. The icon shows Jesus grasping the Torah scroll, indicating that Jesus's teaching is rooted in the Law and the prophets of Israel. His cruciform halo expresses both his sacred cross and his divinity.

Jesus is seated on the royal throne of Israel's kings, expressing the authority that he possesses as the One who inaugurates the kingdom of God. Among the elders in the Temple, Jesus seems to be a learner, "listening to them and asking them questions," but also their teacher, as they are "amazed at his understanding and his answers." We can look at the faces and gestures of the six elders and imagine the ideas and wonder that filled them at this moment. The scene anticipates the end of Jesus's teaching ministry, when he will be found again teaching in the Temple by responding to the questions posed to him by the Jewish leaders (Lk 20–21).

Jesus's height above all the others in the Temple expresses the position of a teacher in ancient times whose disciples listen at his feet. But his elevation also communicates his ultimate destiny that requires his being with his Father. It prefigures the end of the Gospel in which Jesus ascends to the Father in heaven. Even as Jesus is found in the Temple, he has already begun the process of withdrawing from his earthy origins so that he can fulfill his purpose given by the Father.

The position of Mary and Joseph in the icon clearly indicates that they are removed from the main scene. They are outside the semicircle dominated by Jesus and the Temple elders. Mary does not understand what Jesus said about directing his life to the Father, yet she "treasured all these things in her heart." She accepted the words of Jesus and trusted in him. For us, the scriptures and icons do not bring us to full understanding, but they invite us to meditate and contemplate the mysteries in order to perceive their deeper meanings and their implications for our lives.

Meditatio

Now spend some time reflecting on the gospel and the icon, allowing them to interact with your own world of memories, questions, ideas, and aspirations, until you are aware of the personal messages they are offering to you.

- Have you ever been separated from your parents or from your child? Consider what this experience of loss was like for you. What must have been the feelings of Mary and Joseph as they discovered the loss of their son and their frantic search for him?

- Have you ever "lost" Jesus at one or more periods of your life? How did you "find" him again at the center of your life? What has this experience taught you?

- The gospels frequently associate being lost with death and being found with a return to life. At the conclusion of Jesus's parable of the lost son, the father says that he "was dead and has come to life; he was lost and has been found" (Lk 15:32). In what sense does this express the pattern for the Christian life: lost to found, death to life?

- This narrative shows us ways that the family of Jesus, Mary, and Joseph integrated the everyday responsibilities of family life with their life under God's covenant, with its call to worship and serve God. What can you learn from the Holy Family about the joys, challenges, struggles, and blessings of family life?

- At some point in the life of every child, parents realize that their child does not belong to them. Their joy of seeing their child grow up is tempered with the sorrow of knowing that childhood quickly flees. Mary and Joseph experience Jesus in the natural stage of assertive adolescence, but they also realize that their son is called to a life devoted to God's plan. What does the fact that Jesus is both Son of Mary and Son of God teach you about raising children?

- In the third century, the theologian Origen wrote, "Learn from Mary to seek Jesus." In seeking Jesus we discover that his way is different from and beyond all our expectations. Seeking Jesus leads us to new and unexpected discoveries about the ways of God. What have you learned from Mary about seeking Jesus?

Oratio

Respond in prayer to this narrative by imitating the trusting faith and humble acceptance of Mary. Begin with this prayer, then continue to pray in your own words.

- Father, your Son learned that his work was doing your will and that his home was with you. Instill the wisdom of your Spirit within me so that I will do your work and seek my home with you. Help me to imitate your Son so that I may be obedient both to the external commands of your word and to the internal urgings you instill within me. . . .

Contemplatio

Remain in restful quiet, experiencing the invitation offered by the sacred page and holy image. Spend time in the divine presence allowing God to work within you.

- The gospel says that Mary "treasured all these things in her heart." Spend some time allowing your heart to be opened by God's grace and filled with God's word.

Operatio

Lectio and visio divina teach us to experience God's word in ways that move us toward the witness of discipleship. Consider ways this encounter is transforming your thoughts and behaviors.

- The desire of Jesus, Mary, and Joseph to live in accordance with God's will is an inspiration for family life. What are some ways that you might better respond to God's calling within your family? Offer some sign of appreciation for a member of your family.

The Baptism of Jesus

Lectio

Read this gospel text aloud, letting go of your own presumptions and listening to the words as if for the first time. Be aware of your breathing in and breathing out. Call upon the same Holy Spirit who inspired the sacred evangelist to fill your heart and kindle in you the fire of divine love.

Matthew 3:1–2, 10–17

In those days John the Baptist appeared in the wilderness of Judea, proclaiming, "Repent, for the kingdom of heaven has come near." . . .

"Even now the ax is lying at the root of the trees; every tree therefore that does not bear good fruit is cut down and thrown into the fire. I baptize you with water for repentance, but One who is more powerful than I is coming after me; I am not worthy to carry his sandals. He will baptize you with the Holy Spirit and fire. His winnowing fork is in his hand, and he will clear his threshing floor and will gather his wheat into the granary; but the chaff he will burn with unquenchable fire."

Then Jesus came from Galilee to John at the Jordan, to be baptized by him. John would have prevented him, saying, "I need to be baptized by you, and do you come to me?" But Jesus answered him, "Let it be so now; for it is proper for us in this way to fulfill all righteousness." Then he consented. And when Jesus had been baptized, just as he came up from the water, suddenly the heavens were opened to him and he saw the Spirit of God descending like a dove and alighting on him. And a voice from heaven said, "This is my Son, the Beloved, with whom I am well pleased."

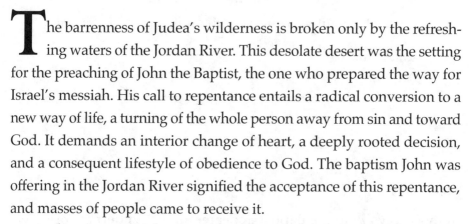

The barrenness of Judea's wilderness is broken only by the refreshing waters of the Jordan River. This desolate desert was the setting for the preaching of John the Baptist, the one who prepared the way for Israel's messiah. His call to repentance entails a radical conversion to a new way of life, a turning of the whole person away from sin and toward God. It demands an interior change of heart, a deeply rooted decision, and a consequent lifestyle of obedience to God. The baptism John was offering in the Jordan River signified the acceptance of this repentance, and masses of people came to receive it.

As the witness of John comes to a close, Jesus makes his first appearance and associates himself with John's call to conversion and immersion into the waters of the Jordan. Jesus was certainly not a sinner who needed to repent, as John acknowledged as he protested his unworthiness to baptize Jesus. God's Messiah came to the river because he embodies the ideal Israel, the People of God who began their life in the land by crossing the Jordan River and entering the new life God had promised them. Jesus was baptized by John to unite himself fully with our humanity so that he could lead us to the fullness of life.

As Jesus is immersed in the water and comes up from the water, his baptism is accompanied by two signs that manifest his true identity: one is seen and the other is heard. The descending dove represents the Spirit of God. After the flood of the book of Genesis, the first sign of God's new creation was a dove, sent out by Noah, who hovered over the waters carrying an olive branch. The dove made known the good news of God's reconciliation and the hope of future grace. As Jesus is manifested to the world in baptism, the Holy Spirit descends upon him as a sign of the new creation coming upon the earth through the saving ministry of Jesus Christ. At the same time, the Father's voice declared Jesus to be his beloved Son.

The gospel announces that the time has come. Through his Son, God is resurrecting the world from its fallen state. We who follow Jesus, who are baptized into him, become beloved sons and daughters of God. Through him the new way is opened between God and the people of the earth.

Visio

Let the icon of Jesus's baptism renew within you the
experience of your own Baptism. Relate the scene and its
visual and auditory signs to the gospel proclamation you
have heard. Let the colors, faces, gestures, and symbols
within the image lead you to a deep encounter with God.

Although John is baptizing Jesus, the baptizer is clearly not the focus of the icon. John is on the left side, bent in reverence to Jesus. He is baptizing but also looking toward heaven in witness to the revelation of God. Near John are his disciples as well as a tree with an ax lying next to it, ready to be cut down. The image expresses the urgency of John's preaching. The tree that does not bear good fruit will be cut down for firewood. The time for repentance is now because God's reign is coming into the world in his Son, Jesus the Messiah. On the right side, bowing in adoration of Jesus, are three angels. Their hands are covered, indicating the sacredness of the body of Jesus. They are ready to receive the newly baptized Jesus as he comes out of the water, to clothe his naked body, and to serve his needs. In the middle is the moment of revelation itself.

The icon of Jesus's baptism presents the Orthodox feast of the Theophany, the feast that reveals the Holy Trinity to the world. In the center is Jesus submerged in the waters of the Jordan River. At the top of the icon a semicircle depicts the opening of the heavens and the hand of God, a visual expression of the voice of the Father declaring Jesus as his beloved Son. Above the head of Jesus is the Holy Spirit descending as a dove upon the Son and resting upon him. The three persons of the Trinity are manifested together: the Father testifying from on high to the divine sonship of Jesus; the Son receiving his Father's testimony; and the Spirit in the form of a dove, animating Jesus for his ministry in the world.

While the other figures are focused on Jesus or the Trinitarian manifestation, Jesus is gazing directly at us. He seems almost as wide as the Jordan River itself, which cuts a path through the rocky and mountainous wilderness on either side. The divinity of Jesus is revealed while he submits himself to the water-baptism of his precursor John. Rather than the waters of the Jordan cleansing Christ, it is he who cleanses the waters. The right hand of Jesus is shown sanctifying the waters of baptism so that we, like the fishes shown in the water around Jesus, may swim in the pure waters of divine life.

Meditatio

Spend some time allowing the gospel and the icon to dialogue with the book and holy image of your own life so that you come to better understand the deep significance of this divine manifestation.

- The preaching of John the Baptist expresses the urgency of the times and warnings of judgment. What seems to be the essence of his call to repentance? Why does he use the image of a fruitful tree to signify a repentant life?

- Jesus insisted on being baptized by John, even though Jesus was sinless and in no need of repentance. He takes on himself the guilt of all people in allowing himself to be lowered into the water. What does this indicate to you about the ministry of Jesus and his solidarity with humanity?

- As Jesus rises from the waters, the heavens are opened, never to be shut again, inaugurating a new age of God's grace and a new relationship between heaven and earth. How does this view of the world express the reality of Christian Baptism and its power to transform lives?

- The exchange between the Father, Son, and Holy Spirit at the baptism of Jesus demonstrates the relationship to which God calls all people. Through Baptism into the Spirit-filled Son of God, we become beloved sons and daughters of God and are commissioned to serve God's kingdom in his name. How does Baptism affect your relationship with God?

- Jesus foreshadowed his death and resurrection as he descended into the waters of John's baptism, taking upon himself the guilt of humanity, and rose from the waters to receive the Holy Spirit. In what ways do you experience your Baptism as a descent and ascent, as a dying and rising with Christ?

- Recall the grace of your own Baptism and realize that God's grace is just as active as on the day of your new birth in Christ. What particular mission is God calling you to as his baptized child?

Oratio

After hearing and seeing God's revelation through the baptism of Jesus, respond to God's revelation with heartfelt and embodied prayer. Let this prayer be an incentive to continue with your own.

- Father, who gave witness to your beloved Son and sent your Spirit upon him at his baptism in the Jordan River, stir up in me the grace of my own Baptism. Send your Spirit to enliven me, guide me with your hand, give me a passion for justice, and make me generous in your service. . . .

Contemplatio

When the words of your prayer begin to seem inadequate, move into wordless contemplative prayer. Realize that the special place that Jesus holds in God's affections has been extended in Baptism to you.

- As followers of Jesus, we are people on whom the waters of Baptism are never dry. Realize that your life is united intimately with the Father, Son, and Holy Spirit. Spend some quiet moments in union with the source of the divine life within you.

Operatio

The practice of lectio and visio divina shows us how to listen with open ears and to see with watchful eyes in a way that makes a difference in our lives. Consider ways that you would like to act on your experience of God's word today.

- Our Christian Baptism calls us to be active disciples of Jesus in the world. In what ways might God be calling you to a more active discipleship through reflection on your Baptism? Choose one thing to do that will outwardly express that you have been baptized into Jesus Christ.

The Wedding at Cana

Lectio

In a quiet and comfortable space, kiss the words of the gospel to prepare yourself to encounter the inspired Word of God. Read the text aloud, listening and seeking its fullest meaning. Use your imagination to picture the scene in your mind and feel the emotions of each character in your heart.

John 2:1–11

On the third day there was a wedding in Cana of Galilee, and the mother of Jesus was there. Jesus and his disciples had also been invited to the wedding. When the wine gave out, the mother of Jesus said to him,

"They have no wine." And Jesus said to her, "Woman, what concern is that to you and to me? My hour has not yet come." His mother said to the servants, "Do whatever he tells you." Now standing there were six stone water jars for the Jewish rites of purification, each holding twenty or thirty gallons. Jesus said to them, "Fill the jars with water." And they filled them up to the brim. He said to them, "Now draw some out, and take it to the chief steward." So they took it. When the steward tasted the water that had become wine, and did not know where it came from (though the servants who had drawn the water knew), the steward called the bridegroom and said to him, "Everyone serves the good wine first, and then the inferior wine after the guests have become drunk. But you have kept the good wine until now." Jesus did this, the first of his signs, in Cana of Galilee, and revealed his glory; and his disciples believed in him.

The first person introduced in this wedding scene is "the mother of Jesus." She is accompanied at the celebration by Jesus and his disciples. Mary sees the problem of the lack of wine, a serious quandary in a culture in which one's honor was measured by the success of such public events as weddings. She calls attention to the dilemma and initiates the action of the scene with her statement to Jesus, "They have no wine." Following what seems to be a sharp rebuke from her son, she determinedly instructs the servants, "Do whatever he tells you." Her words initiate a series of events that lead to the miracle and confidently teach the waiters as well as all those who read the gospel that they should put into action whatever Jesus tells them to do. She is the first person in John's gospel to show that the appropriate response to the presence of Jesus is trusting obedience to his word. Even in the face of seeming rebuke, the mother of Jesus trusts unreservedly in the efficacy of the words of Jesus, becoming in this first of Jesus's miracle accounts the model of a true believer and disciple.

The response of Jesus to his mother, "My hour has not yet come," anticipates the completion of Jesus's "hour," the future glorification of Jesus on the cross. There, when Jesus is "lifted up from the earth" on the cross (Jn 12:32), the mother of Jesus will become the mother of his disciples (Jn 19:26–27). In this sense, the miracle at Cana foreshadows the cross, and the transformed wine prefigures Jesus's gift of himself.

Here in Cana, Jesus finds a way to meet the needs of the hour by performing an unobtrusive miracle. Only Jesus's mother, the chief steward, a few servants, and Jesus's disciples knew what happened. There is no indication that the other guests realized what Jesus had done. By acting discreetly, Jesus saves the host from any embarrassment and avoids stealing the spotlight from the wedding.

In this first "sign" of John's gospel, the emphasis is not only on the quantity of wine—six huge water jars holding water used for the Jewish rites of purification—but also on the quality of the wine: the chief steward told the bridegroom, "You have kept the good wine until now." The "now" is the time awaited by the prophets, the time of fulfillment, the beginning of the Messiah's mission.

Visio

Let the faces and gestures of this gospel narrative draw you into the image. Enter the scene with your mind and heart open to the revelation the icon discloses to you. Imagine the thoughts and feelings of each character, and be grateful for the presence of Jesus and his mother.

The icon contains the multiple characters of the gospel account. Behind the table of the marriage feast are the bride and groom, with their hands together on the table. Around them are family and friends, probably the father of the bride on the right. It seems that there is still plenty of food on the table and the cup of the bride's father still holds wine. But the cup of the friend on the left has run dry, and he is gesturing to the servants for a refill.

In Judaism, wine is an expression of joyful celebration. The prophets of Israel had used images of abundant and quality wine to express the restoration of King David's rule and the coming of the messiah. Isaiah proclaims that "the Lord of hosts will make for all peoples a feast of rich food, a feast of well-matured wines" (Is 25:6). Jesus teaches about the kingdom of God throughout the gospels using images of the wedding feast.

The foreground contains the action of the servants in filling six stone jars with water, as Jesus has asked them to do. Each of the jars are filled "up to the brim." As the jars are filled with water, Jesus transforms the water into wine as Mary looks on, confidently trusting her Son to do what is needed. The mysterious implement with which Jesus touches the water turned to wine is a visual symbol of divine authority or power. The instrument, a *rabdos* in Greek, appeared in early Christian art comparing Moses, who used his staff or rod to part the waters of the sea or to strike the rock in the wilderness, to Jesus, who is depicted as using a similar instrument in performing his miracles. The instrument should be considered a symbol rather than a magical wand, as some have claimed. The amount of wine that fills the jars is abundant by any measure, expressing the fullness of life that Jesus offers.

The disciples of Jesus are not in the icon because the viewers are the disciples. We are challenged to see "the first of his signs" and believe in him. Each sign of John's gospel points beyond the event to the truth about who Jesus is and to the kind of transformed life he offers. For those who believe in him, life will never again be predictable, bland, and colorless like water. Life in him, rather, is rich, vibrant, and invigorating like wine.

Meditatio

Continue meditating on this scene, imagining the sights, sounds, tastes, and smells of the wedding banquet. Consider your own responses to the questions and challenges that this scene presents to you.

- Think about weddings you have attended and the kinds of thoughts and emotions that fill such a celebration. What could be some of the reasons why Jesus chose this setting and this miracle as the first sign to reveal his glory?

- The fact that the mother of Jesus is the first guest mentioned and the initiator of the miracle indicates that her role is crucial to the narrative. In what way does this account portray Mary as a model for the disciples of Jesus?

- Consider any experiences you have shared of wine-tasting or of opening a bottle of fine wine. What does the abundance of fine wine in the miracle at Cana say to you about the characteristics of Jesus's ministry and the quality of life he offers?

- Mary exercises her maternal role in giving birth to the adult ministry of Jesus in this first act of his public life. Just as a mother instinctively knows the time for giving birth and the needs of her child, Mary knew when the time was ready for Jesus to be revealed and she initiated his ministry with her words. How can Mary use her maternal intuition to help you in your life as a disciple of her Son?

- The mother of Jesus tells the servants and all of us, "Do whatever he tells you." What does this instruction say to you about trust, expectancy, and obedience?

- Saint Augustine offers an interpretation of the water and the wine of the wedding as the scriptures of the Old and New Testaments. Jesus could have poured out the water and poured in the wine. But instead Christ showed us that the Old Testament comes from him also because by his orders the jars were filled with water. The whole of the scriptures begin to taste like wine when Christ is understood within them.

Oratio

Respond to this joyful account of the wedding banquet with your own prayer of praise and thanksgiving. Imitate the trusting faith and humble acceptance of Mary as you continue to pray in your own words.

- Lord of the age to come, who transforms water into wine, thank you for manifesting the power of your divine generosity. Transform my life from ordinary existence to abundant living. Help me to do whatever you tell me, and give me a lively hope in the glorious wedding feast you have promised. . . .

Contemplatio

When the words of your prayer begin to seem inadequate and no longer necessary, move into wordless contemplative prayer.

- Imagine that the feasting and celebration of the wedding have ended and the crowd has returned home. Sit in silence and ponder the goodness of God that you have just experienced.

Operatio

Consider ways that you would like to act on your experience of God's word today, and make a commitment to change one aspect of your life.

- What would help you to see the vibrant, abundant possibilities within the ordinary, predictable elements of your life? How can you adjust your vision today?

The Proclamation of God's Kingdom

Lectio

Ask the Holy Spirit to enlighten your mind and heart as you prepare to listen to God's inspired Word. Prepare to place yourself in the scene with all its sights, sounds, smells, tastes, and textures. Imaginatively enter the scene and participate in the narrative on the sea.

Mark 1:14–18, 4:35–41

Jesus came to Galilee, proclaiming the good news of God, and saying, "The time is fulfilled, and the kingdom of God has come near; repent, and believe in the good news." As Jesus passed along the Sea of Galilee, he saw Simon and his brother Andrew casting a net into the lake—for they were fishermen. And Jesus said to them, "Follow me and I will make you fish for people." And immediately they left their nets and followed him. . . .

On that day, when evening had come, he said to them, "Let us go across to the other side." And leaving the crowd behind, they took him with them in the boat, just as he was. Other boats were with him. A great gale arose, and the waves beat into the boat, so that the boat was already being swamped. But he was in the stern, asleep on the cushion; and they woke him up and said to him, "Teacher, do you not care that we are perishing?" He woke up and rebuked the wind, and said to the sea, "Peace! Be still!" Then the wind ceased, and there was a dead calm. He said to them, "Why are you afraid? Have you still no faith?" And they were filled with great awe and said to one another, "Who then is this, that even the wind and the sea obey him?"

Jesus proclaims, "The time is fulfilled." God is breaking into history to carry out his ancient promises and to bring the divine plan of salvation to completion. The heart of Jesus's proclamation of the Good News is this: "The kingdom of God has come near." The term kingdom should be understood in a dynamic sense, not as a territory or place but rather as the "reign of God" that has entered the world with the ministry of Jesus. This kingdom is the world as God has always desired it to be—a world of justice, peace, goodness, and joy. The good news is that now this reign of God is beginning for those who choose to accept it and enter into it.

This decisive coming of God's kingdom demands a twofold response: "Repent, and believe in the good news." Repentance means turning away from everything that hinders God's reign, and belief means accepting it and yielding to everything that God is doing in Jesus Christ. An essential aspect of this acceptance is the call to discipleship. Jesus's words to the two brothers, "Follow me and I will make you fish for people," are a succinct expression of the meaning of discipleship. Their response is immediate, selfless, and total, giving their lives a radically new purpose.

The storm on the sea portrays a sharp contrast between Jesus and his disciples. The disciples are terrified of the wind and the surging sea while Jesus is sleeping in the boat. When they awaken him, he rebukes the wind and commands the sea to be calm. Jesus has already taught about the kingdom of God with his parables and demonstrated the power of God's reign with his healings. Here Jesus demonstrates that God's reign extends over even the strongest powers of nature. These mighty deeds of Jesus show that Jesus has authority over sickness, death, and every element that causes fear.

Jesus teaches his disciples to seek first the kingdom of God, trusting in God's sovereign authority over all of creation. The things of this life that lead us to feel anxious—like food, clothing, work, income, and security—are all important, but they cannot sustain us at the core of our being. When they become the center of our concern, we are left feeling anxious and depleted. When we entrust our lives to God, joining as disciples to seek his reign, our lives find purpose that allows us to live with trusting confidence.

Visio

Fix your eyes on the serene face of Jesus. Let his sovereign authority over the wind and the waves draw you into this scene. Become a part of the community of disciples, letting Jesus lead you to confidence and trust. What do you fear? What do you hope?

Jesus had called all in the boat to follow him and to fish for people. Can you count all twelve in the community of apostles? The haul of fish in the net symbolizes their evangelizing mission, portrayed in scenes on the sea throughout the gospels. Despite their fears on the sea, they are still fishing for people and extending God's reign.

The Sea of Galilee is notorious for its sudden windstorms. They arise without warning, surprising even seasoned seafarers with their terrifying fierceness. The waves are breaking over the boat, and it is filling with water. We can imagine the terror in the disciples as they attempt to row the boat, steady the mast, save the catch, and plead with Jesus for help. Then, with supreme authority, Jesus rebukes the wind and orders the sea to be silent. In the psalms and prophets of Israel, represented by the scroll in Jesus's hand, control over the sea and the calming of storms are characteristic signs of God's power. Here Jesus blesses the world with his right hand and conquers the wind and the waves with his word. The danger is replaced by the complete calm, and the fear of the disciples is transformed into a deeper faith.

On the lips of the disciples is the final question of the text, "Who then is this, that even the wind and the sea obey him?" The icon evokes the same question from us as we ponder the full identity of Jesus. It offers the Church a lesson in trust. At the time of Mark's writing the gospel, the Church was suffering persecution. The scene urges the early Church of Mark and disciples in every age to cast away their doubts and trust in the divine power of Jesus over all opposing forces.

The boat became an early symbol for the Church in Christian art. The icon emphasizes this with the mast, which is shaped like the cross, and with the blowing sail, which reminds us of the winding sheet of Jesus left in his empty tomb. The Church, like the barque on the sea, is safely guided by Jesus through the storms of this world. The Gospel and the icon teach disciples in every age that, although Jesus allows storms and trials to come, nothing can ultimately harm those who place their trust in him.

Meditatio

Allow the inspired text and sacred image to interact with your own world of memories, fears, distresses, and hopes. Let God's word become a living word for you, seeing its personal message and meaning.

- Jesus came to bring the kingdom of God into the world. It is present here, but we await its full manifestation. In what ways did Jesus demonstrate the coming of God's reign through his life and ministry?

- Jesus's words "Follow me and I will make you fish for people" are a succinct expression of the meaning of discipleship. What fishing skills are required for effective discipleship? In what ways does following Jesus lead you to fish for people?

- Simon and Andrew responded to the call of Jesus by immediately leaving their nets. What attachments, fears, or wants must you leave behind in order to place Jesus and the kingdom first in your priorities?

- Why does Jesus ask, "Why are you afraid?" when fear seems like a natural response in a storm? What are some of your own deepest fears? In what way do your fears hold you back and prevent you from living life in abundance?

- What might be some of the reasons why the boat was used in early Christian art as a symbol of the Church? What are some of the storms that the Church faces today? What does the image of Jesus and his disciples in the boat teach you about these storms?

- Meditate on the words of Psalm 107:23–32, a psalm of thanksgiving for God's help in a time of trouble and fear. In what ways is it similar to the gospel narrative of the storm at sea? In what ways does this psalm give you comfort and help you to trust?

Oratio

Respond in prayer to the words and images you have experienced. Begin with these words and then continue with your own prayer of petition, repentance, thanksgiving, and praise.

- Master of the Sea, who calms the wind and the waves, hear my prayer in distress. I am overwhelmed by life's storms and the swirling chaos around me. Give me assurance that you can quiet the wind and calm the waves. Take away my fears and help me to trust in you. . . .

Contemplatio

Dispense with all words and images; calm your mind and emotions. Just rest in God as you move to contemplative prayer.

- Imagine that Jesus has answered your plea for help and has calmed the storm around you. Visualize yourself in the boat on a calm and sunny day or lying on the shore. Simply accept the grace of this moment, with your mind and heart at ease.

Operatio

Decide how you will let this time of prayer and reflection change you and help you to follow Jesus as an effective disciple for God's kingdom.

- How would you live if you were free from fear, trusting in God's sovereignty over your life? Why not begin to live that way now? Choose one way you want to change as a result of this experience of lectio and visio divina.

The Transfiguration
of Jesus Christ

Lectio

Be still in mind and body as you prepare to experience God's transforming Word. Breathe slowly, calling on the same Holy Spirit who filled the sacred writers to fill your heart. Read the text aloud, seeing the text with your eyes, vocalizing the text with your lips, and hearing the text with your ears.

Mark 9:2–10

Six days later, Jesus took with him Peter and James and John, and led them up a high mountain apart, by themselves. And he was transfigured before them, and his clothes became dazzling white, such as no one on earth could bleach them. And there appeared to them Elijah with Moses, who were talking with Jesus. Then Peter said to Jesus, "Rabbi, it is good for us to be here; let us make three dwellings, one for you, one for Moses, and one for Elijah." He did not know what to say, for they were terrified. Then a cloud overshadowed them, and from the cloud there came a voice, "This is my Son, the Beloved; listen to him!" Suddenly when they looked around, they saw no one with them anymore, but only Jesus.

As they were coming down the mountain, he ordered them to tell no one about what they had seen, until after the Son of Man had risen from the dead. So they kept the matter to themselves, questioning what this rising from the dead could mean.

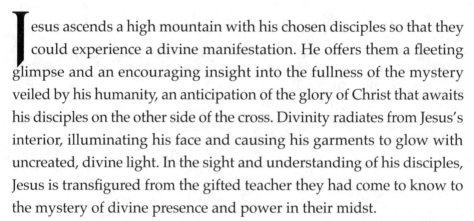

Jesus ascends a high mountain with his chosen disciples so that they could experience a divine manifestation. He offers them a fleeting glimpse and an encouraging insight into the fullness of the mystery veiled by his humanity, an anticipation of the glory of Christ that awaits his disciples on the other side of the cross. Divinity radiates from Jesus's interior, illuminating his face and causing his garments to glow with uncreated, divine light. In the sight and understanding of his disciples, Jesus is transfigured from the gifted teacher they had come to know to the mystery of divine presence and power in their midst.

Moses and Elijah, representing the Torah and the prophets, embody the whole of God's revelation to Israel. As they appear with the transfigured Jesus on the mountaintop, this vision expresses a climactic moment in God's saving mission for the world. During their earthly lives, both Moses and Elijah traveled to other mountains to experience the glory of God. Those encounters with God would sustain them on their obedient journeys of faith and suffering for the People of God (Ex 19, 1 Kgs 19). Jesus follows in their way and brings their saving path to its glorious culmination.

Peter, James, and John are caught up in an awesome and holy encounter that they cannot adequately articulate. The mystery must be contemplated rather than described. Peter's instincts are correct in suggesting he erect "three dwellings" on the spot. The word indicates the temporary, makeshift shelters erected during the Jewish feast of Sukkoth to remember Israel's forty-year journey through the desert. Peter's remembrance of the saving path of the Exodus is a recognition that we are indeed the people of the way, on the path of discipleship.

From the overshadowing cloud, God reveals the identity of Jesus to the disciples: "This is my Son, the Beloved." God's voice then commands the disciples, "Listen to him!" As they come down the mountain, Jesus and his disciples begin their journey to Jerusalem, a passage that will lead to the cross. Peter, James, and John must listen to what Jesus teaches them as they follow in his way. They must not speak about what they have seen until the Resurrection. Only in light of the climax of Jesus's life, represented by the cross and the empty tomb, could people begin to understand his transcendent glory.

Visio

Gaze upon the transfigured image of Jesus and let it lead you to a divine encounter. Let each figure teach you something about how to trust and follow Jesus. Let the uncreated light of the icon illumine your heart with God's grace.

People throughout the scriptures often climb mountains to experience a divine manifestation. According to the ancient view of the cosmos, God dwells above the heavens, so going to a high mountain expresses the human effort to draw near to God. The cloud that covers the mountain from which the divine voice speaks, in turn, expresses God's coming down to the human level. The encounter with the divine, then, is the process of both the ascending human and the descending divine, expressing the joining together of human effort and divine grace.

The glorified Christ is the center and focus of the image, his hand held in a blessing, eyes directed at us. His clothes are "dazzling white," and the cloud overshadowing the scene is indicated by the mandorla around his body. This is an ancient symbol of two circles coming together and partially overlapping one another to form an almond shape in the middle. Early Christian art used the mandorla to symbolize the coming together of heaven and earth, spirit and matter, the human and divine. From the luminous body of Christ, shafts of golden light radiate toward the five other figures present.

Next to Christ but on different peaks of the mountain are Elijah on the left and Moses on the right holding the book of the Torah. These three serene and splendid figures at the top are contrasted with the three frightened and confused disciples at the bottom of the icon. Peter is gesturing toward Christ and speaking about erecting three dwellings, John seems to have fallen backward at the vision, and James is shielding himself from the brightness. As we gaze at the icon, we are with the disciples, seeking to understand and appreciate the vision. The Transfiguration is not only an event for us to witness, but also a process in which we should partake. The graced vision has been given to us through God's revelation, but we must make the effort to open ourselves to the experience of being transformed.

For us, as for the disciples, the Transfiguration is a brief experience of unity: heaven with earth, spirit with matter, our humanity with God's divinity. So the mandorla is the divine container in which new creation begins to form and germinate. The Transfiguration points toward the final glory of Christ, the fulfillment of God's kingdom when all creation will be transfigured and filled with light. As we learn the way of spiritual ascent, we experience more frequent and deeper encounters with Christ, where at the summit, those shafts of divine light can penetrate us, too.

Meditatio

God's voice told the disciples to "listen" to Jesus, a process that requires a silent, receptive mind and heart. They had to learn how to temporarily suspend their own assumptions and let go of some of their mental defenses in order to truly learn from him. Reflect on this biblical scene until you are led to deeper understanding.

- In the Transfiguration scene, God reveals the most important personages of the Old Testament to the most significant individuals of the gospels. What does the Transfiguration teach you about hoping in God's saving plan, trusting in God's will, and following in God's way?

- The Christian life is largely a matter of seeing well, with clearer and fuller vision. God washes out our eyes again and again, with tears of sorrow and tears of joy, so that we can see better. Are you able to see the glory of God's presence shining in the lives of people around you? What would give you clearer vision?

- The icon describes the divine encounter as a combination of human effort and divine grace. In what ways do you experience your prayerful encounters with God as a joining of effort and grace?

- The mandorla in which Christ is enshrined expresses unity in the midst of our ordinary experience of duality. How can you more fully realize that you are part of God's new creation and experience this unity more often?

- In the biblical languages, "to listen" means both to hear and to obey. God tells the disciples to listen to Jesus as he teaches them the way of discipleship on the journey toward Jerusalem. As you reflect on God's command "to listen" to Jesus, what are you being challenged to believe or to do?

- Transfigurations in our own lives might be described as those moments in which our hearts are able to "see" a much fuller reality

and meaning than what our eyes can see. What are examples of
transfigurations that you have experienced? When have you come
to appreciate the world as charged with the grandeur of God?

Oratio

*Prayer begins by truly listening to God's word and is followed by meditation
on that word until its truth leads to deep understanding. When you are ready
to respond to God's word in prayer, begin with these words.*

- Glorious Lord, who was transfigured on the mountain to reveal
  your glory to your disciples insofar as they could comprehend, illuminate me with your everlasting light. Cleanse my eyes to help
  me see and enkindle the spark of divinity in me and those around
  me. . . .

Contemplatio

The Transfiguration is filled with quiet awe. Spend some silent moments allowing God to be present in your innermost being.

- Imagine the cloud of God's presence overshadowing you on the mountaintop. Rest in that image, and experience the majesty of God and the divine presence surrounding you. Open yourself to whatever kind of transfiguration God desires to work within you.

Operatio

As you prayerfully reflect on scripture, God's word gradually but surely transfigures you into a greater expression of Christ in the world. Consider how you will express your transformed life through Christlike actions.

- After the Transfiguration of Christ, the disciples descended the mountain with Jesus in order to travel with him to Jerusalem. In what ways has your prayerful experience of God's word illumined you and prepared you for the journey ahead?

The Last Supper

Lectio

Prepare your physical space and your inner spirit to listen and receive the Word of God. Dedicate this time for sacred conversation with God. Ask the Holy Spirit to help you to truly listen and to guide your response to the inspired page.

Matthew 26:19–30

So the disciples did as Jesus had directed them, and they prepared the Passover meal. When it was evening, he took his place with the Twelve; and while they were eating, he said, "Truly I tell you, one of you will betray me." And they became greatly distressed and began to say to him one after another, "Surely not I, Lord?" He answered, "The one who has dipped his hand into the bowl with me will betray me. The Son of Man goes as it is written of him, but woe to that one by whom the Son of Man is betrayed! It would have been better for that one not to have been born." Judas, who betrayed him, said, "Surely not I, Rabbi?" He replied, "You have said so."

While they were eating, Jesus took a loaf of bread, and after blessing it he broke it, gave it to the disciples, and said, "Take, eat; this is my body." Then he took a cup, and after giving thanks he gave it to them, saying, "Drink from it, all of you; for this is my blood of the covenant, which is poured out for many for the forgiveness of sins. I tell you, I will never again drink of this fruit of the vine until that day when I drink it new with you in my Father's kingdom." When they had sung the hymn, they went out to the Mount of Olives.

After sunset, as Passover began, Jewish families would gather in Jerusalem to remember the saving events that made them God's people and to rededicate themselves to their covenant with God. In the Passover meal, they also looked forward to the redemption that God had continually promised them through the prophets. This Passover would be the last meal Jesus would share with his disciples before his death.

Although sharing this meal is the greatest Jewish expression of communion in God's covenant, Jesus reveals a terrible breach of loyalty: "One of you will betray me." He emphasizes the heinous nature of the betrayal by noting that the culprit is one of the Twelve, "the one who has dipped his hand into the bowl with me." The treachery seems to echo a psalm of lament: "Even my bosom friend in whom I trusted, who ate of my bread, has lifted the heel against me" (Ps 41:9). We are drawn into the shocked response of the disciples. One by one they ask,

"Surely not I?" We must each repeat the question in turn. Each of us must recognize the evil of which we are capable, realizing that any one of us could potentially prove unfaithful in a similar way.

At this last supper, Jesus gave a radically new meaning to the food and drink of the sacred meal: "Take, eat; this is my body. . . . Drink from it, all of you; for this is my blood of the covenant." Consecrated and sanctified, the bread and wine become the Body and Blood of Christ. This change is not physical but mystical and sacramental. In the eucharistic meal, Christ feeds us with his own being, so that we might become "participants in the divine nature" (2 Pt 1:4).

In the Eucharist, the Church sacramentally reenacts the redemptive event of Christ's cross and participates in its saving grace. The body of Christ is sacrificed and his blood is "poured out for many for the forgiveness of sins." We come to this great sacrament to experience over and over the mystery of salvation and to be united intimately to the passion and resurrection of Jesus Christ. In the Eucharist we receive and partake in his sacrificed, risen, and deified body for our eternal life. It constantly renews and increases our new life in Christ. As the center of the Church's life, the Eucharist is the Church's principal activity and most profound prayer.

Visio

Gaze upon this image and let it draw you into the scene.
Fix your eyes upon the faces and gestures of Jesus and
his apostles. Imagine the thoughts and emotions of the
scene, and let them lead you into an encounter with the
eucharistic Christ.

The icon portrays Christ gathered with his twelve disciples around a table on the evening of Passover. It includes details mentioned in all four of the gospels. The scene captures the moment immediately after Jesus announced, "One of you will betray me" (Jn 13:21–27). We see that the apostles are looking in different directions, puzzled and "uncertain of whom he was speaking." The beloved disciple, traditionally said to be John, leans into Jesus, because the fourth gospel tells us, "One of his disciples—the one whom Jesus loved—was reclining next to him." The figure in the middle of the icon, gesturing toward John and Jesus, is Simon Peter. The same gospel tells us that Peter motioned to John to ask Jesus of whom he was speaking.

The most dramatic action is shown by the motion of Judas the betrayer, stretching his hand toward the bowl. Judas is so close to Jesus, and yet so far away. He has become part of a conspiracy that within a few hours will result in the arrest, trial, torture, and execution of Jesus. The bowl reminds us of another bowl the next morning in which Pilate will wash his hands of responsibility for his actions. No one wants to take upon himself the blame for the murder of Jesus. Immediately behind the figure of Judas is an open door. Jesus says to him, "Do quickly what you are going to do." And Judas immediately went out into the night.

Jesus understood the hearts of those gathered with him. Although he knew their hidden intentions, Jesus never forced anyone's response to him. Like these disciples, we are free to love the Lord, as John does, or to betray the Lord, as does Judas. We are free to choose. There is space at the Lord's table for all who desire to be there and to follow Christ. In the Orthodox tradition, this final meal before Christ's death is not called the Last Supper but rather the Holy Supper or sometimes the Mystical Supper. It is not the disciples' last meal with Jesus because there will be many more. Despite the fact that Peter will deny him that night and all the others will flee in fear, the resurrected Lord will gather with all his disciples in the Church's Eucharist. At the table of God's kingdom, Jesus is present with us and his self-gift for us continues.

Meditatio

Meditation has been described as chewing on the sacred text in order to under-
stand it more fully. Ruminate on the inspired Word you have heard and the
holy icon you have looked upon until you become aware of the nourishment
being offered to you.

- The Passover meal is the final meal of Jesus with his disciples before his passion and death. In what ways does Israel's Passover
help you to understand the meaning of his holy supper and the
new covenant it commemorates?

- The icon of the holy supper highlights the love of John for Jesus
and the betrayal of Jesus by Judas. In what ways do these actions
by John and Judas lead you to ponder the icon and consider its
implications for your own life?

- The holy supper of Jesus is filled with betrayal, anguish, and dread
about what lay ahead, but it is also a feast of great joy, longing, and
hope for what God has promised. In what ways do you understand the Eucharist as the culmination of the whole life of Jesus?

- In Jesus's gift of the Eucharist, he offers his body, which is given
up for us, and his blood, which is poured out for the forgiveness of
sins. What do you think about when you say "amen" while receiving the body and blood of Christ in Communion?

- Every liturgy of the Church participates in Christ's eternal offering
of himself to the Father. In what ways is this holy sacrifice and
mystical meal the greatest gift of Christ to his Church?

- Lectio divina has been compared to the process of eating God's
word: taking a bite (lectio), chewing on it (meditatio), delighting in
its flavor (oratio), digesting it to become part of the body (contemplatio), and metabolizing it so that it may be put to use in forms of
witness and service (operatio).

Oratio

Delight in the flavor of God's word as you pray in response to the sacred text you have pondered and the holy icon you have gazed upon.

- God of the covenant, who has united us to your Son through the everlasting Sacrament of his Body and Blood, free us from the bondage of sin and death. In the midst of the snares and temptations that abound in the world around and in us, help me to live in communion with everything that is good, noble, and worthy, being formed by your grace into the image of your Son Jesus Christ. . . .

Contemplatio

Digest the Word of God as it becomes part of your own life, letting it move from your lips and tongue into your heart.

- Choose a word from the text or an image from the icon to bring into the silence of contemplation. Focus on the word or image and allow God to work deeply within you, transforming you into a more complete divine image.

Operatio

Metabolize God's word so that it may be put to use in forms of witness and service.

- Let this experience of hearing the inspired text and seeing the icon of the Holy Supper lead you to a deeper appreciation of the sacrament of the Eucharist. What is one thing you would like to enhance about your own participation in the eucharistic liturgy of the Church?

The
Agony of Jesus

Lectio

We all know what it feels like to be sleepy and unable to stay awake. Drowsiness can influence our discipleship and prevent us from being watchful and ready for the many aspects of Christ's coming to us. Open your mind and heart to listen carefully to God's voice speaking to you through the gospel.

Matthew 26:36–46

Then Jesus went with them to a place called Gethsemane; and he said to his disciples, "Sit here while I go over there and pray." He took with him Peter and the two sons of Zebedee, and began to be grieved and agitated. Then he said to them, "I am deeply grieved, even to death; remain here, and stay awake with me." And going a little farther, he threw himself on the ground and prayed, "My Father, if it is possible, let this cup pass from me; yet not what I want but what you want." Then he came to the disciples and found them sleeping; and he said to Peter, "So, could you not stay awake with me one hour? Stay awake and pray that you may not come into the time of trial; the spirit indeed is willing, but the flesh is weak." Again he went away for the second time and prayed, "My Father, if this cannot pass unless I drink it, your will be done." Again he came and found them sleeping, for their eyes were heavy. So leaving them again, he went away and prayed for the third time, saying the same words. Then he came to the disciples and said to them, "Are you still sleeping and taking your rest? See, the hour is at hand, and the Son of Man is betrayed into the hands of sinners. Get up, let us be going. See, my betrayer is at hand."

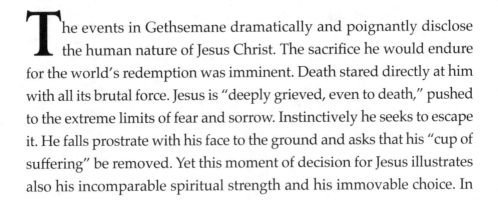

The events in Gethsemane dramatically and poignantly disclose the human nature of Jesus Christ. The sacrifice he would endure for the world's redemption was imminent. Death stared directly at him with all its brutal force. Jesus is "deeply grieved, even to death," pushed to the extreme limits of fear and sorrow. Instinctively he seeks to escape it. He falls prostrate with his face to the ground and asks that his "cup of suffering" be removed. Yet this moment of decision for Jesus illustrates also his incomparable spiritual strength and his immovable choice. In the same breath in which he asked that his suffering be removed, he prayed to his Father, "Not what I want but what you want."

Jesus remained in prayer that night, although he could have easily escaped his arrest and passion by continuing up and over the Mount of Olives and into the Judean wilderness. But, while he felt a natural aversion and horror at the prospect of a painful death, Jesus was completely willing to embrace that suffering for the sake of his love for humanity and to carry out his Father's plan for the world's salvation. He willingly took upon himself the sin of humanity and agreed to carry it to the cross. Christ's obedience in the Garden of Gethsemane reverses the disobedience of Adam in the Garden of Eden. During Adam's time of testing in the garden, he failed to trust the Father, preferring his own will to God's. But during the testing of Jesus, he trusted completely and was intent on faithfulness to the Father. Adam's "no" to God led him to the forbidden tree; Jesus's obedient "yes" led him to the wood of the cross, the new tree of life.

The fervent prayer of Jesus is strongly contrasted with the disciples' behavior. Three times Jesus returns from prayer to find them asleep. Their three lost opportunities to stay alert anticipate Peter's three opportunities to confess his discipleship that night. But each time he was asked in the courtyard of the high priest after Jesus's arrest, he denied knowing Jesus. The posture of discipleship must be watchfulness and readiness if followers of Jesus are to continue his mission despite opposition. Jesus's counsel to "stay awake and pray" summons all disciples not to grow weary and lax, but to be alert to the agony of Christ, in whatever person or situation, in whatever time and place.

Visio

Gaze upon the icon as it invites you into the scene. Imaginatively enter into the space of the one open-eyed disciple. Consider what he is seeing, hearing, thinking, and feeling as Jesus alternately prays in agony and speaks to the disciples.

The icon clearly portrays two levels of Jesus's agony in Gethsemane. At the top, we see Jesus with hands outstretched. He is praying to the Father, symbolized by the familiar divine hand extended from heaven. In Luke's version, Jesus prays, "Father, if you are willing, remove this cup from me; yet, not my will but yours be done." We also see an angel near Jesus, also with outstretched hand. The gospel says, "Then an angel from heaven appeared to him and gave him strength" (Lk 22:42–43). The Father has offered him an emissary from the divine realm to sustain him in the final struggle.

Below we see Jesus in the bright garden speaking with his disciples, who are in a black cave in the olive grove. As with the Holy Supper, we notice a contrast between loyalty and betrayal, obedience and neglect, light and darkness. Jesus is praying fervently to the Father while his disciples lie sleeping, unable to stay awake despite his urgent requests that they "stay awake and pray." Because they grow drowsy and slumber, they will not be prepared for the time of trial.

How many disciples are sleeping in the darkness? Judas is in total darkness, leading those who will arrest Jesus and ready to betray him with a kiss. Peter seems to be the only disciple whose eyes are at least momentarily open, hearing the warnings of Jesus about being watch-ful and alert. The gospel narrative showing the failures of the original twelve disciples teaches future disciples. "The spirit is indeed willing, but the flesh is weak," Jesus warns. This battling spirit and flesh will continue to clash in the lives of all disciples. In the womb-like darkness of the cave, these eleven disciples are still growing and developing through the trials of Jesus's agony and their horrible mistakes during his passion. But through the new birth of Christ's resurrection, these slumbering neophytes will emerge as chastened and wiser disciples to lead his Church.

The icon of Christ's agony forms a sharp contrast with the icon of the Transfiguration. In both of these episodes, Jesus took his closest disciples with him to reveal the depth of his mission. As the disciples had witnessed Jesus in glory on the mountaintop, they now see him in anguish in the olive grove. If we are to truly understand Jesus, we must, like those original disciples, meditate on his human agony as well as his divine glory.

Meditatio

The challenge of meditation is to continue reflecting on the biblical narrative and the icon until they become a mirror in which we see our own reflection. Try to recognize within the inspired text and image your own temptations, sins, challenges, and failures, and seek to learn from them.

- Jesus did not flee from his suffering but remained in prayer. He accepted his death, not with a kind of stoic passivity and resignation, but as an act of the highest form of love. His absolute self-giving broke the power of death, with all of its attendant fears and anxieties. In what ways does the agony of Jesus guide you in the face of suffering and death?

- Although Jesus is fully divine, he is human in every way. Divesting himself of divine prerogatives, the Son of God assumed the role of a servant. As a man, he was destined to fully experience the human condition, including suffering and death. In what ways is your faith enriched by considering the ways that Jesus experienced struggles similar to your own?

- Gazing upon the icon of Jesus's agony, reflect on the contrast between the prayer of Jesus and the sleep of his disciples. What does the icon teach you about watchfulness and its importance for the Christian life?

- Imaginatively place yourself in the scene of Jesus's agony, considering the sights and sounds, thoughts and emotions. What do you notice? How do you feel? How might this scene change your heart?

- Contrast your experience of the icon of the Transfiguration with the icon of Jesus's agony. What are the similarities and differences you notice? Why are both icons necessary for a full contemplative experience of Jesus?

- The commands of Jesus to his disciples in the olive grove of Gethsemane seem to parallel different movements of lectio divina. Jesus says to them: "Sit here," "Remain here and stay awake," "Stay awake and pray," and "Get up." How do these imperatives guide you in your practice of lectio, meditatio, oratio, contemplatio, and operatio?

Oratio

Staying awake in prayer, begin to respond to the experiences of hearing and seeing God's word. Give voice to the response that arises from within you.

- My Father in heaven, may your will be done on earth as it is in heaven. Help me to stay watchful and alert, so that I may be prepared for the hour of trial. I want to live in obedience to you, to submit my will to your own, and to entrust my life into your hands. . . .

Contemplatio

When the words of your prayer begin to seem inadequate and no longer necessary, move into wordless contemplative prayer.

- Placing yourself beside Jesus in the grove of olives, seek to join your heart to his. Remain here in silent contemplation, accepting the transforming grace God desires to give to you.

Operatio

Get up from your prayerful experience with the Lord, resolved to change some aspect of your discipleship as a result.

- Staying watchful is a strong theme during the Orthodox liturgy for Holy Week: "Behold the Bridegroom comes at midnight, and blessed is the servant whom he shall find watching, and unworthy is the servant whom he shall find heedless" (Troparion for Bridegroom, Matins). What could you do to incorporate a deeper sense of vigilance into your relationship with God?

The
Flagellation of Christ

Lectio

Breathe slowly, calling on the same Holy Spirit who filled the gospel writer to fill your heart. Begin reading when you feel ready to hear God's voice. Read this passion narrative as if for the first time, trying to let go of your own presumptions so that you can listen to God speaking to you anew.

Matthew 27:22–31

Pilate said to them, "Then what should I do with Jesus who is called the Messiah?" All of them said, "Let him be crucified!" Then he asked, "Why, what evil has he done?" But they shouted all the more, "Let him be crucified!" So when Pilate saw that he could do nothing, but rather that a riot was beginning, he took some water and washed his hands before the crowd, saying, "I am innocent of this man's blood; see to it yourselves." Then the people as a whole answered, "His blood be on us and on our children!" So he released Barabbas for them; and after flogging Jesus, he handed him over to be crucified.

Then the soldiers of the governor took Jesus into the governor's headquarters, and they gathered the whole cohort around him. They stripped him and put a scarlet robe on him, and after twisting some thorns into a crown, they put it on his head. They put a reed in his right hand and knelt before him and mocked him, saying, "Hail, King of the Jews!" They spat on him, and took the reed and struck him on the head. After mocking him, they stripped him of the robe and put his own clothes on him. Then they led him away to crucify him.

The flagellation of Jesus with whips is a powerful expression of the multiple torments Jesus experienced during the hours of his passion. While the gospels mention only briefly that Jesus was flogged before being handed over for crucifixion, readers knew the familiar details of scourging as well as the particulars of crucifixion. The writer's mention that Jesus was flogged at the hands of Pilate and his Roman soldiers convinced readers that Jesus endured the most brutal of tortures.

Beatings with wooden rods or leather whips were a severe punishment in the ancient world. The Torah stated that the number of lashes should be proportionate to the offense and that the maximum number applied to a victim was forty, so as not to degrade the person being punished (Dt 25:2–3). Jewish practice subtracted one stroke to guarantee that the limit would not be surpassed, and "forty lashes minus one" (2 Cor 11:24) became characteristic of Jewish punishment. Roman floggings, however, bore no such restrictions and were generally far more brutal. Often the straps of leather used for Roman scourges were weighted at the ends with pieces of metal or bone, which would rip the victim's flesh. Prisoners to be scourged were usually stripped and tied to a pillar. The flagellation often served as a prelude to crucifixion, inflicting intense physical trauma and weakening the prisoner, resulting in a quicker death.

The custom of releasing a prisoner at Passover seems to have been a concession to the Jews, a conciliatory gesture on the part of the Roman government. Nationalistic fervor ran high during the feast of Israel's liberation, and allowing the Jews to choose a prisoner for release was meant to cool their passions. The choice between Jesus or Barabbas rested with the crowd, though they were prompted by the chief priests to call for Barabbas. The release of Barabbas, followed by the crucifixion of Jesus, expresses how Jesus takes our sins upon himself so that we might go free and live. Barabbas's name literally means "son of the father." We are all the Father's sons and daughters, who have been freed and given life by the true Son, Jesus Christ.

Pilate reluctantly hands Jesus over for crucifixion, symbolically washing his hands in a pathetic gesture trying to rid himself of responsibility. Pilate, however, is the only figure who can authorize a crucifixion, and he must share the guilt for Jesus's death.

Visio

Look at the painful scene depicted in this icon. Fix your

eyes upon the faces and gestures of each person in the

scene. Relate the elements of the scene to the sacred

scriptures you have heard. Consider the thoughts and

emotions of those looking upon this scene.

T he icon portrays one of the many moments of suffering from the
passion of Christ. The brutal lashings that Jesus endured at the
hands of the Roman soldiers are given only the briefest mention in the
gospel accounts. Yet, the flagellation has become a focus of Christian art
because of the way the prophet Isaiah described the suffering of God's
servant and the meaning of that suffering for the sake of God's people.
The servant was "despised and rejected." He was stricken, smitten, and
afflicted (Is 53:3–4). The servant exclaims, "I gave my back to those who
struck me" (Is 50:6). Yet, the servant is innocent and his suffering is for
the sake of others: "He was wounded for our transgressions, crushed for
our iniquities" (Is 53:5). He is a vicarious sufferer, taking upon himself
the suffering that others deserved. As a result of his ordeal, others are
healed and made whole.

The gospels demonstrate that Jesus fulfills the prophecy of God's Suffering Servant in Isaiah. The prophet includes us all when he announces,
"All we like sheep have gone astray; we have all turned to our own
way, and the Lord has laid on him the iniquity of us all" (Is 53:6). As
the sins of God's people were laid on the sin offerings in the Temple
and on the scapegoat on the Day of Atonement, our sins have been laid

on the Suffering Servant of God. In him our sins find forgiveness, our brokenness is made whole, and our spiritual illness is healed.

So the icon expresses not only the physical torment of Jesus as he is scourged by the Roman soldiers. It expresses also, and more importantly, the meaning of that suffering of Christ. Jesus is afflicted with the whips of the Roman system, but his wounds are for the sake of our healing. As we see the lashings at the hands of the soldiers, we realize that he is wounded for our transgressions and that he has taken upon himself our iniquities.

Pilate is clothed in regal attire, while Jesus has been stripped. The Roman governor is seated on his authoritative throne, while the Messiah is tortured with brutal lashes. And although Christ seems helpless, he remains crowned with the halo of divinity and sanctity. The scene expresses the wonderful paradox that Jesus is the wounded healer, the sacrificed Messiah, the suffering Lord.

Meditatio

Allow the book of your life and the inspired scriptures to dialogue so that you come to understand the significance of this gospel scene for your own discipleship. Consider what aspects of your own life experiences are highlighted by the gospel text and the icon.

- Jesus accepted the penalty for the crimes of Barabbas. How would you feel if you were Barabbas—guilty yet set free? In what sense are you Barabbas?

- What physical, mental, and emotional tortures do the soldiers inflict on Jesus? Why is the icon more concerned with the meaning and significance of these events rather than just the suffering itself?

- The icon includes the figures of Mary and others, looking on from a distance as Jesus is struck and humiliated. Consider the emotions and responses of these disciples peering from outside of Pilate's court. Why does the iconographer choose to hide their faces?

- Christ is a wonderful physician; he heals by taking the sicknesses of his people upon himself. Through his suffering and his cross he has redeemed the world. In what ways are you grateful that Christ is a wounded healer, a sacrificed Messiah, and a suffering Lord?

- Why is our world so saturated with violence, hostility, and rage? In what ways does this scene of Jesus's flagellation express the aggression of those who inflict suffering on others? In what ways do you compromise your beliefs or remain silent in the face of injustices?

- Directly behind Jesus in the icon is an open door leading into the darkness. Isaiah the prophet said of God's servant, "By a perversion of justice he was taken away" (Is 53:8). Ponder the exit of Jesus after his scourging, as he is led from Pilate's court into the darkness of his passion and death.

Oratio

Allow yourself to be disturbed and challenged by these words and images. After listening to what the Lord wants to say to you, consider what you want to say in response.

- Suffering Messiah, who was mocked, tormented, and handed over to crucifixion, I cringe in horror at the injustices done to you by those whose lives were controlled by anger and rage. Have mercy on me in your steadfast love, forgive my transgressions, and heal me from the effects of my sin. . . .

Contemplatio

When the words of your prayer begin to seem inadequate, trust in God to work deep within you in ways you do not anticipate or understand.

- Imagine yourself exiting the door with Jesus into the darkness. Realize that sounds and images are not necessary to experience the divine presence. Remain here in prolonged silence. Place yourself in God's care.

Operatio

Consider ways that you would like to act on your experience of God's word today, and make a commitment to change one aspect of your life.

- As you realize the darkness that is around you and within you, what can you do to challenge the world's deceit? Into what dark corner of your life or your community can you let Christ's light shine?

Here Is the Man

Lectio

Be still in mind and body as you prepare to experience the inspired Word. Try to experience with your imagination all the sights, sounds, thoughts, and emotions that fill the text. Read the text aloud, seeing the text with your eyes, vocalizing the text with your lips, and hearing the text with your ears.

John 19:5–16

Jesus came out, wearing the crown of thorns and the purple robe. Pilate said to them, "Here is the man!" When the chief priests and the police saw him, they shouted, "Crucify him! Crucify him!" Pilate said to them,

"Take him yourselves and crucify him; I find no case against him." The Jews answered him, "We have a law, and according to that law he ought to die because he has claimed to be the Son of God."

Now when Pilate heard this, he was more afraid than ever. He entered his headquarters again and asked Jesus, "Where are you from?" But Jesus gave him no answer. Pilate therefore said to him, "Do you refuse to speak to me? Do you not know that I have power to release you, and power to crucify you?" Jesus answered him, "You would have no power over me unless it had been given you from above; therefore the one who handed me over to you is guilty of a greater sin." From then on Pilate tried to release him, but the Jews cried out, "If you release this man, you are no friend of the emperor. Everyone who claims to be a king sets himself against the emperor."

When Pilate heard these words, he brought Jesus outside and sat on the judge's bench at a place called The Stone Pavement, or in Hebrew Gabbatha. Now it was the day of preparation for the Passover; and it was about noon. He said to the Jews, "Here is your king!" They cried out, "Away with him! Away with him! Crucify him!" Pilate asked them, "Shall I crucify your king?" The chief priests answered, "We have no king but the emperor." Then he handed him over to them to be crucified.

The painful humiliation Jesus experienced during his passion was one of the deepest dimensions of his suffering. After Pilate had Jesus flogged, the Roman soldiers mocked him as the King of the Jews. For a diadem they pressed a crown of spiked thorns into his skull, and they sarcastically dressed him in a royal robe. Irony pervades the scene because what the soldiers say and do bespeaks a profound truth about the kingly dignity of Jesus. He is indeed worthy of their homage, but the true nature of his kingship is hidden in lowliness and suffering.

Because Pilate's condemnation of Jesus was under coercion and against his better judgment, he attempts to minimize the significance of Jesus with mockery. Pilate solemnly displays Jesus to his opponents outside with the words, "Here is the man." Here is Jesus, broken in body, shaking in torturous pain, looked upon with scorn and derision, laughed at and mocked, bloody and beaten, stripped of dignity and identity. This is the history of our cruel humanity, what we do to one another, sin incarnated in Christ's body and blood. This is what hatred, arrogance, and violence does to human beings. Looking at Jesus forces us to look and see what we do to the least of our brothers and sisters.

Although Jesus seems a pitiful and broken man who should not be taken seriously, the true kingship of Jesus was never more clearly displayed. But neither the Roman political authority nor the Jewish religious authority is able to recognize the truth that stands before them. They cannot recognize genuine royal power in the pathetic figure of Jesus, so they seek to destroy what they cannot understand. The Roman governor proclaims his own power, saying to Jesus, "Do you not know that I have power to release you, and power to crucify you?" The chief priests and Temple police shout, "Crucify him!"

Pilate is a cowardly official who abdicates his responsibility, a vacillating judge who allows himself to be swayed by others. When Pilate states, "I find no case against him," the religious leaders play their trump card. "If you release this man you are no friend of the emperor," they shout. By setting Jesus free, Pilate would risk his position as Roman procurator because anyone who claims to be king opposes the emperor. Now "more afraid than ever," Pilate ironically proclaims the truth about Jesus—"Here is your king!"—while handing him over to be crucified.

Visio

Look into this image and let the icon draw you into the encounter. Look upon the faces of each person and consider the ideas and feelings within their minds and hearts as Jesus is presented to the crowd.

Who is responsible for the suffering of Jesus? Is it the religious leaders who plotted against him, the disciple who betrayed him with a kiss, the armed soldiers who seized him in Gethsemane, the disciples who deserted him, the Roman procurator who handed him over to please the crowd, the soldiers who scourged him, or those who hammered in the nails? Jesus suffered because of human sin. The betrayal of Judas, the hatred of the Temple professionals, the cowardice of Pilate, the cruelty of the Romans: this is why Christ appears as he does. What form of humanity is not represented in this image? The cry of the crowd, "crucify him," is the cry of our humanity as it rejects again God's saving love.

Though assaulted and disgraced, still Jesus stands before us. In our infidelity and betrayal, Jesus loves us to the end. This is divine love: "While we were still sinners Christ died for us" (Rom 5:8). Such perfect and complete love casts out fear and guilt. The icon shows us nothing more than what Pilate and the Roman soldiers saw. It is up to us to see deeply, beyond the brutalized man set before us, to see the Savior who burns with love for us. Can we look upon our humiliated king and still worship him as Lord?

In the curtained archway behind Pilate, his wife gasps at the sight. Matthew's gospel tells us that she sent a message to her husband: "Have nothing to do with that innocent man, for today I have suffered a great deal because of a dream about him" (Mt 27:19). Both Jews and Romans took dreams seriously, as a means of divine communication. The dream of Pilate's wife revealed to her the truth about Jesus, so this Gentile woman interceded to try to save the life of the Jewish Messiah.

Yet her intercession was ultimately unsuccessful as her vacillating husband gave in to the pressure of the crowd. The gospel doesn't tell us what happened to Pilate's wife, either immediately after the crucifixion of Jesus when she encountered her husband again or the direction of her life from then on. Although her pleas for Jesus hint at the later tradition that holds that she became a follower of Christ.

Pilate is shown washing his hands, a dismal gesture seeking to disassociate himself with the death of Jesus. How often do we wash our hands of responsibility for the sins of the world? The icon invites us to repentance.

Meditatio

Meditate on this scene from the passion of Jesus from the midst of your own darkness, confusion, struggles, and indecisions. Consider God's saving work in your life and how you can receive the revelation of divine truth and accept God's divine love.

- Pilate is shown to be waffling in his responsibilities as judge. What seems to be Pilate's overriding concern in the trial of Jesus? What do you do to appease the crowds?

- Pilate and the Romans are just as responsible for the suffering of Jesus as the religious leaders among the Jews. In what ways does this scene demonstrate how impossible it is to blame the crucifixion of Jesus on any one group of people?

- What might be some of the motivations of Pilate's wife in urging her husband to have nothing to do with the murder of this innocent man? What does her witness tell you about the importance of defending and suffering for the truth?

- After the death of Jesus "suffered under Pontius Pilate," what might be part of the conversation between Pilate and his wife? What can you learn and imitate from her witness?

- The power brokers of politics, religion, and industry believe that their strength and intimidation of others solves problems. They weigh human life on the scales of convenience. In what ways is the reign of Christ totally different than the kingdoms of this world? What are characteristics of the power of Jesus's realm?

- Pilate ironically proclaimed the truth about Jesus while presenting him to the authorities outside with the words, "Here is your king!" How is the reign of Christ demonstrated in this scene? Why are his opponents unable to recognize his royal authority? In what ways does the world still fail to see God's reign manifested in him?

Oratio

Offer to God what you have discovered in yourself from your meditation. Begin your prayer with these words and then continue in your own words.

- King of heaven and earth, whose source of power is divine truth manifested in love, reign over my life. Help me to claim the power you have given me, and help me to use that power for your glory. . . .

Contemplatio

When the words of your prayer begin to seem inadequate and no longer necessary, move into wordless contemplative prayer.

- When Pilate brought Jesus outside to the crowd, he said, "Here is the man!" Look upon the face of Jesus and let God lead you to repentance for your share in the world's sin.

Operatio

Consider ways that you would like to act on your experience of God's word today, and make a commitment to change one aspect of your life.

- In his passion, Jesus teaches us the source and the characteristics of true power. Genuine power is exercised in love and used to serve others. How might I claim the power God gives me and use the power of God's kingdom for the good of the people around me?

Carrying the Cross

Lectio

Prepare yourself to enter personally into this gospel passage as you imagine the sights, sounds, scents, and textures of the scene. Read the sacred page aloud, seeing the text with your eyes, vocalizing it with your lips, and hearing it with your ears.

Luke 23:26–34

As they led him away, they seized a man, Simon of Cyrene, who was coming from the country, and they laid the cross on him, and made him carry it behind Jesus. A great number of the people followed him, and among them were women who were beating their breasts and wailing for him. But Jesus turned to them and said, "Daughters of Jerusalem, do not weep for me, but weep for yourselves and for your children. For the days are surely coming when they will say, 'Blessed are the barren, and the wombs that never bore, and the breasts that never nursed.' Then they will begin to say to the mountains, 'Fall on us'; and to the hills, 'Cover us.' For if they do this when the wood is green, what will happen when it is dry?"

Two others also, who were criminals, were led away to be put to death with him. When they came to the place that is called The Skull, they crucified Jesus there with the criminals, one on his right and one on his left. Then Jesus said, "Father, forgive them; for they do not know what they are doing."

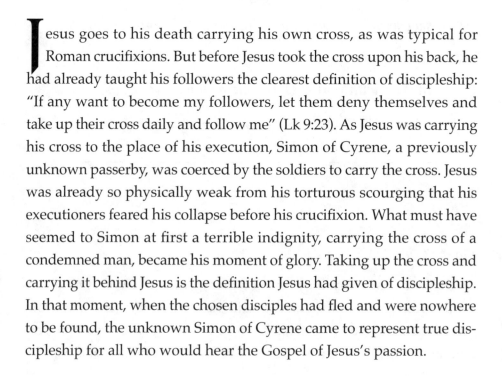

Jesus goes to his death carrying his own cross, as was typical for Roman crucifixions. But before Jesus took the cross upon his back, he had already taught his followers the clearest definition of discipleship: "If any want to become my followers, let them deny themselves and take up their cross daily and follow me" (Lk 9:23). As Jesus was carrying his cross to the place of his execution, Simon of Cyrene, a previously unknown passerby, was coerced by the soldiers to carry the cross. Jesus was already so physically weak from his torturous scourging that his executioners feared his collapse before his crucifixion. What must have seemed to Simon at first a terrible indignity, carrying the cross of a condemned man, became his moment of glory. Taking up the cross and carrying it behind Jesus is the definition Jesus had given of discipleship. In that moment, when the chosen disciples had fled and were nowhere to be found, the unknown Simon of Cyrene came to represent true discipleship for all who would hear the Gospel of Jesus's passion.

Freed from carrying the cross, Jesus turns to address the women who were also following him and lamenting his crucifixion. They represent the people of Jerusalem and become recipients of Jesus's prophecy of the city's destruction. The women are mourning for Jesus, but Jesus tells them that they should be mourning for themselves and their children. Using several proverbs, Jesus describes the sufferings of Jerusalem's fall. First, the usual blessedness of bearing children is reversed, and the barren are declared blessed. Second, people will desire a quick death, begging the mountains and hills to collapse upon them. Third, Jesus compares his own suffering to green wood, which is difficult to kindle, and the suffering of Jerusalem to dry wood, which is easy to kindle and to be consumed in fire. If Jesus who is innocent has experienced so much suffering, how much suffering awaits the guilty of Jerusalem.

Jesus's compassion is reflected in all the events surrounding his death. He even prays for his executioners, asking the Father to forgive them. Certainly this prayer is for the Roman soldiers carrying out the details of crucifixion, but it must also be for the religious leaders and all in the crowd whose pleas brought Jesus to the cross. Truly no one knew the significance of what they were doing.

Visio

Look into the scene, noticing the Roman soldiers leading
Jesus and also the women and other inhabitants of Jeru-
salem following him. Then look into the face of Jesus as
he embraces his cross and walks through the city gates.
Enter into the icon with hesitation and humility, seeking
to walk behind Jesus on the way.

I n accord with Roman custom, Jesus had to carry his own cross to the place of execution. The figures in the icon look toward Jesus, but Jesus looks directly at us. Because, in one form or another, this way of the cross is everyone's way. That's why Jesus, loving us to the end, took the way of the cross ahead of us. When we experience the inevitable burdens, afflictions, sufferings, and losses of life, we can look to Jesus who walked the Via Dolorosa, the sorrowful journey, in front of us.

Roman crucifixions took place outside the walls of the city, but usually along a major road leading from the city so that crowds could witness what happened when someone dared to revolt against the authority of the empire. The way of the cross led from the place of Jesus's trial, through the city gate, to the place called The Skull. The icon shows us the walls and gate of the city. Earlier that same week Jesus had royally entered the gates of Jerusalem, with the whole multitude praising God and welcoming "the king who comes in the name of the Lord" (Lk 19:38). Now Jesus exits the city gate, staggering and humiliated. Some of the multitude were weeping and mourning his sufferings; others were shouting mocking insults.

In bearing the cross, Christ submits to everything each of us fears and out of fear seeks to avoid: rejection, condemnation, humiliation, pain, failure, and death. He does so freely, with no motive but love for those with whom he became one in the flesh. No one has greater love, Jesus taught, than to lay down his life for his friends.

The image shows Jesus with the inhabitants of Jerusalem, some women of the city, and his own mother. They are weeping over him, but Jesus tells them to weep for themselves and their children. He is grieved not for his own suffering and pending death but for the horrible suffering that would soon come upon the city of Jerusalem. Because they would reject the kingdom Jesus came to bring and choose the path of insurrection over the way of nonviolence, the road to rebellion over the way of the cross, their city would soon be destroyed by the armies of Rome. Rather than focus on the anguish of Jesus alone, he himself recommends that we ponder his cross in solidarity with our own burdens and with suffering people everywhere.

Meditatio

As you walk in the way of the cross with Jesus, reflect on his suffering and his self-giving love. Consider what personal message and challenges the inspired text and icon offer to you.

- Jesus's way of the cross is our way, too. What are some of the ways in which Jesus demonstrates his solidarity with suffering humanity through the way of his cross?

- What might Simon of Cyrene have felt as he was made to carry the cross of Jesus? In what way has he become an image of true discipleship? How might he have been changed forever on that fateful day?

- Even Jesus needed someone to help him with his cross. When have you found it difficult to carry your cross? Who helped you carry your cross or made its burden easier?

- Throughout his life, Jesus had taught his disciples to forgive the faults and sins of others. At the end of his life, Jesus prays, "Father, forgive them; for they do not know what they are doing." For whom is Jesus asking forgiveness? What challenge does his example offer to you?

- Unlike the images of Western art, the icon does not express the physical suffering of Jesus. Rather, it leads us deeper into the motivations of his heart and the significance of his actions. What is the most impressive thing for you about the character Jesus showed during his sorrowful passion?

- In speaking to the women of Jerusalem, Jesus seeks to divert their sorrow from himself to the sufferings that would come upon themselves, their families, and the inhabitants of their city. How does your heart change as you ponder his cross in solidarity with your own burdens and with suffering people everywhere?

Oratio

Pondering the cross of Jesus leads us to respond with prayers of lament and hope. United with the mother of Jesus and the women of Jerusalem, pray the prayer that arises from your heart.

- Suffering Lord, who shows us the way to salvation through the self-surrender of the cross, teach me to take up the cross and follow after you each day. As I follow in your footsteps, teach me to walk in solidarity with your suffering people everywhere. . . .

Contemplatio

The passion of Jesus and his love for us leads to silent wonder and awe at the gift of his cross. Let your reflection and prayer lead you to wordless contemplation.

- Look into the face and eyes of Jesus as he carries his cross along the way. Let his mercy transform your heart, and let him give you the gift of compassion.

Operatio

Actualize God's words by putting into action in your daily life the insights and transformation of heart you have received by pondering the sacred page.

- Rather than focusing on the suffering of Jesus alone, he himself recommends that we ponder his cross in union with the sufferings of others. How can you develop a greater solidarity with those in need by reflecting on the cross of Jesus?

The
Crucifixion

Lectio

Hold a cross, light a candle, kiss the sacred text, or perform some other action to help you remain focused. Breathe slowly, calling on the same Holy Spirit who filled the sacred writers to fill your heart. Read the text slowly and aloud.

John 19:19–30

Pilate also had an inscription written and put on the cross. It read, "Jesus of Nazareth, the King of the Jews." Many of the Jews read this inscription, because the place where Jesus was crucified was near the city; and it was written in Hebrew, in Latin, and in Greek. Then the chief priests of the Jews said to Pilate, "Do not write, 'The King of the Jews,' but, 'This man said, I am King of the Jews.'" Pilate answered, "What I have written I have written." When the soldiers had crucified Jesus, they took his clothes and divided them into four parts, one for each soldier. They also took his tunic; now the tunic was seamless, woven in one piece from the top. So they said to one another, "Let us not tear it, but cast lots for it to see who will get it." This was to fulfill what the scripture says, "They divided my clothes among themselves, and for my clothing they cast lots." And that is what the soldiers did. Meanwhile, standing near the cross of Jesus were his mother, and his mother's sister, Mary the wife of Clopas, and Mary Magdalene. When Jesus saw his mother and the disciple whom he loved standing beside her, he said to his mother, "Woman, here is your son." Then he said to the disciple, "Here is your mother." And from that hour the disciple took her into his own home.

After this, when Jesus knew that all was now finished, he said (in order to fulfill the scripture), "I am thirsty." A jar full of sour wine was standing there. So they put a sponge full of the wine on a branch of hyssop and held it to his mouth. When Jesus had received the wine, he said, "It is finished." Then he bowed his head and gave up his spirit.

The crucifixion of Jesus is the climax of his passion and the threshold to his glory. The scene is both tragic and triumphant. The gospels do not offer an extended description of Jesus's torturous death; the agony of crucifixion was widely known. Rather, the gospels focus on the nobility and significance of Christ's death. This is life lived with love to the end, even to death on a cross. In the ancient Roman world, parents who passed by the road lined with crosses would say to their children, "See, that's what happens to people when they live a bad life."

But Jesus transformed the cross from a hated instrument of punishment to a glorious sign of saving love. Now Christian parents who point out the cross to their children say, "See, that's how much God was willing to do for you to show his love."

A majestic God, insulated in the heavens and isolated from human struggles and pain, would not seem very reliable or convincing in our suffering world. But God entered into our world of flesh and blood, tears and death. The cross is our most powerful reminder that God is with us even in pain, tragedy, and seemingly hopeless situations. In every moment of suffering and death, we can find our God. He has borne and transformed our humanity and our mortality, and so we are saved now, even from the clutch and dread of death. In looking at Christ crucified we see the saving love of God expressed most conclusively.

On the cross Jesus had to let go, first of his possessions, even his clothing, then of his family, even his mother, and finally of life itself. The evangelist comments that "Jesus knew that all was now finished," indicating that Jesus knew that his mission on earth was complete. The words of Jesus, "I am thirsty," express a physical thirst but also a thirst for his final union with the Father, as proclaimed at the beginning of Psalm 63: "Oh God, you are my God, I seek you, my soul thirsts for you." And so Jesus uttered his final words: "It is finished." As he died, the text tells us, Jesus "gave up his spirit." More than a mere euphemism for death, the words indicate that Jesus poured out his Spirit upon the infant Church gathered at the cross. As he let go of his own life, he breathed life into the newborn community of faith.

Visio

Gaze upon the image of Christ crucified and let it invite you into a participation in the holy mystery of the Lord's saving death. Place yourself beneath the cross with the women and men who look upon Jesus as he bows his head and delivers over his spirit.

The icon of the crucifixion does not emphasize the blood, bruises, and agony of Christ's torturous death but concentrates on the more hidden dimensions of the event. The stress is on Christ's gift of himself. The holy and life-giving cross expresses both the vertical and horizontal dimensions of Christ's sacrifice. Above the crucified Lord is the divine hand, representing the Father's acceptance of Christ's self-emptying love. The sun and moon express the cosmic dimensions of his eternal sacrifice, with its redeeming effects on all of creation. The prophet Joel, quoted by Peter at Pentecost, declared, "The sun shall be turned to darkness and the moon to blood" (Acts 2:20), symbolizing the end of an era. Beneath the cross, the hill of Golgotha is split by an earthquake at the death of Christ and a skull is revealed. An early tradition held that Jesus was crucified at the place where Adam was buried, again expressing the significance of Christ's death. Adam represents sinful humanity, but Christ is the new Adam, the firstborn of our new humanity redeemed from sin and its consequences.

The cross in the Orthodox Church is shown with three vertical bars. The top bar represents the sign nailed to the cross, declaring the crucifixion as a royal enthronement: "Jesus of Nazareth, the King of the Jews."

The bottom bar is the footrest. Across the middle and longest vertical bar stretch the arms of Christ, which embrace the world.

The figures beneath the cross represent the beginnings of the Church. The pangs that give birth to the Church are the sufferings of Christ because from his passion are born future generations of Christian believers. In the final act of his life, Jesus forms a new family at the cross, a family born not of blood but of faith. The two figures closest to Jesus are his mother and "the disciple whom he loved." Jesus entrusts his mother to his beloved disciple and the disciple to his mother. From that moment, Mary gained the filial care of a new son and all disciples gained Mary as their faithful mother. The other male figure is the Roman centurion, who at the death of Jesus declared him to be the Son of God. The other women are Mary Magdalene and Mary the wife of Clopas. Together they form the Church in miniature, enlivened by the life-giving blood and water that flow from Christ's side.

Meditatio

Having listened carefully to scripture and gazed attentively at the icon, seek to assimilate them in all their depth so that you can respond to them with your life.

- In Eastern art, the crucified and deceased Jesus is shown with the halo of divinity, whereas in Western art, he is more often depicted wearing a crown of thorns. What might be some reasons for this difference? What are the advantages of portraying Christ either with a crown of suffering or a crown of glory?

- The first Christians would be amazed that the cross, an abrasive symbol of cruelty and violence, would one day become an object of jewelry sold in stores across the world. Do you choose to wear the cross for decoration or devotion? What does it mean to you to use the cross as jewelry?

- As you imagine yourself in the place of each of the major characters at the foot of the cross, what is your experience? With which of these characters can you best relate?

- Pope Leo the Great urged Christians not to let the eyes of their mind dwell only on the scene of crucifixion as it was seen by sinners, but to let their understanding see the glory of the cross as seen by the angels and the saints. What happens when you let your mind be illumined by the deeper truth of the cross as seen from heaven?

- In what sense is the last breath of Jesus on the cross also the first breath of his newborn Church? What does this understanding tell you about the nature of the Church and your place within it?

- At the cross, the sword that Simeon had prophesied would pierce Mary's soul (Lk 2:35) struck its deepest wound. But at that moment, Jesus gave Mary as a tender mother to his disciples. How does Mary's maternal care and guidance help you to follow in the way of her Son?

Oratio

Respond in prayer to God's word to you, including the ideas, images, and vocabulary of scripture to enrich the content of your prayer.

- We adore you, O Christ, and we praise you because by your holy cross you have redeemed the world and brought your Church to life. Guide your people to always seek the sacramental graces that flow from your pierced side, and continue to breathe your Spirit into us so that we may be your beloved disciples. . . .

Contemplatio

When the words of your prayer begin to seem inadequate and no longer necessary, move into wordless contemplative prayer.

- Sit or stand beneath the cross of Jesus, experiencing no greater love than his self-offering for you. Rest in his presence and simply accept the grace God wishes you to receive in these moments.

Operatio

Lectio and visio divina gradually but ultimately transform you into a greater expression of the mystery of Christ. Consider ways that you are being changed from within through this ancient practice.

- At the crucifixion, Christ's self-emptying love transformed an instrument of violent torture into the life-giving cross. Choose one way that you can unite yourself with the cross of Christ by giving of yourself in order to bring fuller life to another.

The
Resurrection

Lectio

Approach this sacred text with expectant faith, trusting that God wishes to transform your heart with the power of his Word. Read aloud, seeking to hear God's Word within the page, without any presumptions.

Matthew 27:50–53; 28:1–9

Jesus cried again with a loud voice and breathed his last. At that moment the curtain of the Temple was torn in two, from top to bottom. The earth shook, and the rocks were split. The tombs also were opened, and many bodies of the saints who had fallen asleep were raised. After his resurrection they came out of the tombs and entered the holy city and appeared to many. . . .

After the Sabbath, as the first day of the week was dawning, Mary Magdalene and the other Mary went to see the tomb. And suddenly there was a great earthquake; for an angel of the Lord, descending from heaven, came and rolled back the stone and sat on it. His appearance was like lightning, and his clothing white as snow. For fear of him the guards shook and became like dead men. But the angel said to the women, "Do not be afraid; I know that you are looking for Jesus who was crucified. He is not here; for he has been raised, as he said. Come, see the place where he lay. Then go quickly and tell his disciples, 'He has been raised from the dead, and indeed he is going ahead of you to Galilee; there you will see him.' This is my message for you." So they left the tomb quickly with fear and great joy, and ran to tell his disciples. Suddenly Jesus met them and said, "Greetings!" And they came to him, took hold of his feet, and worshiped him.

The death of Jesus and his resurrection is the climax of human history, the demarcation between the old era of salvation and the new and final age of grace. The crucifixion scene in Matthew's gospel ends with a series of dramatic, apocalyptic signs. The earthquake, the opening of tombs, the raising up and appearance of the saints are all events prophesied for the end of the age. The quaking of the earth indicates the shaking of the old world and the breaking in of God's kingdom. The splitting of the rocks and the liberation of the holy ones from their rock tombs alludes to Ezekiel's prophecy: "You shall know that I am the Lord, when I open your graves, and bring you up from your graves" (Ez 37:13). The earthquake at Golgotha and at the empty tomb ties together the death and resurrection of Jesus into one great final event marking the new and final age of salvation. Although its magnitude shakes the very foundations of the earth, its impact is not destructive, but life-creating and hope-inducing. The death and resurrection of Jesus brings forth a new people, yet God does not forsake or leave behind the saints of ancient Israel but raises them to share in the new life of the kingdom.

The Son of God descended into our fallen humanity in order to raise us up to share in his divinity. In his incarnation and birth, he lowered himself into our world to become flesh and dwell with us. In his public life, he continued to descend, journeying deeply into the lives of humanity's outcasts. By meeting them at their lower points, he healed them, forgave them, delivered them from evil, and restored them to life. Jesus descended most completely into our suffering and sinfulness on the cross. And meeting us there, at the bottom of humanity, Jesus transforms our human nature and lifts it up with him in resurrection.

We see in Jesus what God has promised for our destiny—resurrection from the dead and the fullness of life forever. Yet the resurrection of Jesus is not just good news for our future. In his resurrection, the future already invades the present. Death can already be mocked as a defeated enemy. Christ's resurrection offers us a power for living to overcome even the most difficult obstacles and a purpose for living that assures us that everything we do in his name has eternal consequences.

· LA RÉSURRECTION ·

Visio

Kiss or touch the icon, or let the light of a candle cause its gold to glisten. Let the image draw you into the scene so that you can stand with the saints of old as the glorious Christ lifts them from the abode of death. Let the uncreated light of the icon illumine your heart with God's grace.

The center of Christian faith is Jesus Christ risen from the dead. As such, the feast of Pascha is the most ancient and the greatest of all the many feasts of the Church's liturgical year. This icon of the Resurrection is not content with showing Christ at the empty tomb. Rather, it demonstrates his complete victory over the power of death, conquering its darkness and lifting up all who are trapped in death's abode. As Orthodox Christians chant throughout the Easter season, "Christ is risen from the dead/Trampling down death by death/And upon those in the tombs bestowing life!"

The icon visualizes Christ's descent into Sheol, the dark place reserved for those who died before his victory. They are not forgotten but are raised up to life with him. Christ is shown in his divine glory, surrounded by the mandorla of light, breaking the gates of the underworld that held the dead in captivity. Locks, keys, hinges, and nails float in the darkness, symbolizing that the power of death to imprison God's people is now destroyed.

Christ is lifting up from the darkness the ancestors of humanity, Adam and Eve. These two archetypal figures represent all people who have been offered eternal life through the victory of Christ. Pulling them by the wrist rather than the hand expresses their dependence on him and their inability to climb out themselves. Humble surrender to his divine power is all they are able to do and all they need to do. Also being rescued are the saints of the old covenant. To the left of the icon are John the Baptist and another prophet of old, holding the scroll of prophecy. To the right are Israel's kings, represented by David and Solomon. These representative figures stand for all those who have died before Christ's conquest, and the scene expresses the full reality of what Christ's death and resurrection accomplished.

Christ's descent to the abode of the dead is the first facet of the meaning of his resurrection. His conquest of the power of death is celebrated on Holy Saturday, before the celebration of Christ's manifestation to the disciples. As Saint John of Damascus wrote, "When he had freed those who were bound from the beginning of time, Christ returned from among the dead, having opened for us the way of resurrection." With the People of God we rejoice, "He is risen; he is risen indeed."

Meditatio

Spend some time reflecting on the impact of the Resurrection on your own existence and on the life of the world. Consider how you are being transformed in light of your own personal quest for truth, goodness, and beauty.

- The gospel texts of the death of Jesus and his resurrection are surrounded with apocalyptic signs. What are the meanings of these signs? How do they challenge you to consider the fuller meaning of these saving events?

- Both in the first century and also today, speculators suggest any number of naturalistic explanations for the phenomena associated with the resurrection of Jesus. How would you argue against the idea that the disciples stole the body of Jesus and devised a resurrection hoax? What is the clearest indication to you of Christ's resurrection?

- The entire life of Jesus is described in the gospels as a descent into the depths of humanity. What is the lowest point in my life to which Jesus has descended? How has he lifted me up to share new life in him?

- The women went to the tomb "as the first day of the week was dawning," and they experienced an earthquake as the angel rolled back the stone from the tomb and sat upon it. How do these movements of the sun and the earth express the significance of Christ's resurrection?

- When given their mission by the angel, the women went away from the tomb "with fear and great joy." Is it possible to experience the emotions of both fear and joy simultaneously? When have you felt both great joy and deep fear?

- In what way does the icon of Christ's victory seem richer and a more complete expression of Christ's resurrection than other Easter images you have seen? As you gaze upon it, what hope does it offer to you?

Oratio

After allowing the Resurrection text and icon to touch your heart and stir you to a more vigorous faith, express your personal response in prayer. Begin with this prayer, then continue to pray in your own words.

- Risen Lord, the first to experience God's new creation, descend into the darkness of my life and destroy the fears and powers of death within me. Lift me up to share in your victory, and give me a joyful hope of the world to come. . . .

Contemplatio

It is God's grace working within your heart that gives you a deep desire to rest in the divine presence. Drawing on that desire within you, enter into wordless contemplation of the mystery of resurrection.

- Place yourself in the darkness of the underworld and let Christ be your saving light. Simply accept the transformative graces God wishes to offer you in these moments.

Operatio

The Word of God can change us, shape us, and move us toward a transformed life. Consider what God is doing within you to move you to a more joyful life.

- The light of God's Word dispels the darkness of fear, doubt, and disillusionment. What was one of the main thoughts that arose in you during your listening and gazing? What newness, growth, or movement have you noticed within yourself as a result of your prayerful reflection today?

The Ascension

Lectio

Approach these texts with expectant faith, trusting that God wishes to transform your heart with the power of his Word. Listen to them without prejudgment, hearing them in a new way, guided by God's renewing Spirit.

Acts 1:8–11; Hebrews 9:24–28

[Jesus said] "You will receive power when the Holy Spirit has come upon you; and you will be my witnesses in Jerusalem, in all Judea and Samaria, and to the ends of the earth." When he had said this, as they were watching, he was lifted up, and a cloud took him out of their sight. While he was going and they were gazing up toward heaven, suddenly two men in white robes stood by them. They said, "Men of Galilee, why do you stand looking up toward heaven? This Jesus, who has been taken up from you into heaven, will come in the same way as you saw him go into heaven."

For Christ did not enter a sanctuary made by human hands, a mere copy of the true one, but he entered into heaven itself, now to appear in the presence of God on our behalf. Nor was it to offer himself again and again, as the high priest enters the Holy Place year after year with blood that is not his own; for then he would have had to suffer again and again since the foundation of the world. But as it is, he has appeared once for all at the end of the age to remove sin by the sacrifice of himself. And just as it is appointed for mortals to die once, and after that the judgment, so Christ, having been offered once to bear the sins of many, will appear a second time, not to deal with sin, but to save those who are eagerly waiting for him.

The Ascension represents a moment of transition in the New Testament, the movement from the story of Jesus to the story of the Church. In the writings of Luke, it expresses the shift from his gospel to his Acts of the Apostles. The disciples recognize that the One who has taught, healed, and loved them will no longer be seen by them, but will be present nonetheless. The writer uses a spatial image to express this reality: "He was lifted up, and a cloud took him out of their sight." Yet, we must avoid a simplistic understanding of Jesus's movement, as if he simply launched into space. The fuller meaning is beyond what can be visually seen or verbally expressed.

Hebrews teaches us that Jesus entered into the celestial sanctuary, the heavenly counterpart to the earthly Temple. There Jesus offers the sacrifice of himself for the sin of the world. Because he is beyond the bounds of time and the repetition required for sacrifice in the earthly Temple, Jesus is continually offering his eternal sacrifice. He is continually interceding for us through the "once for all" sacrifice he offered on the cross. Through the Church's eucharistic liturgy, his perfect sacrifice is made present and efficacious for us in every time and in every place in the world.

While Jesus reigns in the heavenly temple, his earthly work continues in the Church until he returns. Jesus has given his disciples a mission. When the Spirit comes upon them, they will be witnesses of Jesus, first in Jerusalem, then in the neighboring regions, and then "to the ends of the earth." But they must wait for the power of the Spirit, because the same Spirit who empowered Jesus will be present in his Church.

Moses and Elijah, who appeared with Jesus at his Transfiguration, each transmitted their "spirit" to their successors at their departure. Because Moses had laid his hands on his successor, Joshua was filled with wisdom and did as God had commanded Moses (Dt 34:9). Before Elijah ascended into heaven, Elisha asked for a double share of his spirit. So when Elijah departed, his spirit became active in his successor. Likewise, when Jesus departs, he promises the Holy Spirit to his Church, so that his saving work will continue in the world. The two men in white robes warn the disciples not to "stand looking toward heaven" because they have a task ahead of them—the evangelization of the world.

Visio

Let the icon invite you in to ponder the scene. Place yourself among the confused and questioning disciples. Consider the mandate of Jesus for his Church and the words of the angels in white. Let the face of Mary offer you wisdom to comprehend the meaning of the mystery.

The icon reveals more than the eye can see, inviting us into a fuller understanding of the Ascension of Christ. The holy image does more than tell the story in a picture. It evokes from us a deeper grasp of the mystery, a better comprehension of Christ's heavenly ministry, and a desire to join the disciples in the work of the Church.

The upper part of the icon presents the glorified Christ. The partial circle, which in previous icons revealed the hand of the Father, is now seen as a full sphere. This divine orb now completely encloses Jesus, expressing his heavenly abode. The mandorla, the almond-shaped intersecting part of two circles as seen in the Transfiguration icon, is now a complete sphere. The duality of matter and spirit, of human and divine, heaven and earth, is resolved and unified in the glorified Christ. The orb represents the glory and majesty of Christ beyond what can be physically witnessed by the gathered disciples and beyond what can be expressed even in the inspired words of scripture. Christ is the new creation, the fullness of which we will experience when Christ comes in glory.

The lower part of the icon portrays the disciples in confusion and wonder. In their midst stand the two men in white robes. Although they point upward, their message to the disciples points them outward toward their mission as witnesses to the ends of the earth. The message that Jesus will return in the future is always given in the context of an exhortation to be about the work of discipleship now. In the center stands Mary, the mother of the disciples and of the Church. She is not staring upward but lovingly toward us. There is serenity in her face and acceptance in her gestures. She understands better than ever the mysteries of her Son's birth, death, and resurrection, already hoping for his return. This hope gives her true wisdom and peace, shared by Christ and the angels in white.

The icon depicts the timeless Church. Although Paul was not yet a Christian at the historical moment of the Ascension, he is present in the icon, the figure just to the right of Mary and the angel. He is the counterpart to Peter on the left. They are the two pillars in Acts, and along with the other ten apostles, they represent the disciples in transition, crossing over from their life with Jesus to the beginnings of the Church.

Meditatio

The Ascension teaches us to ponder the absence of Jesus's physical presence and his new and abiding presence with his Church. Think about the examples of Mary and the apostles as you seek to participate in the mission Jesus gave to his Church.

- The final words of Jesus before his Ascension tell his disciples that the Holy Spirit is coming upon them and that they will be his witnesses to the ends of the earth. In what ways is the Church expressing these words of Jesus today?

- The text of Hebrews expresses the goal of Christ's Ascension in a timeless way. He entered into heaven "to appear in the presence of God on our behalf." In what ways does Christ intercede "on our behalf"? How do the words of Hebrews deepen your understanding of the Ascension?

- The disciples in the icon are presented in a state of transition and confusion, shown by their gestures and the fact that they are not portrayed with halos. What might be some of the reasons for their confusion and lack of order and harmony?

- Contrast the disciples of the icon to the image of Mary. She wears a halo, stands directly beneath the image of Christ, and is the only figure looking directly at us. She is not only mother of the Savior, the bridge that brought divinity to humanity, but now she is also mother of his Church, bringing humanity to divinity. What are some ways that Mary fulfills her role as mother in your own life?

- In what ways do the text and icon of the Ascension confirm, modify, or overturn your understanding of the purpose and mission of the Church?

- Both Moses and Elijah ended their work on earth by passing on their own spirit to their successors. In what sense does Jesus complete this pattern? In what ways does the Acts of the Apostles express this reality?

Oratio

Place your own heart in the heart of Mary, asking for her guidance. Let her lead your prayerful response to God's word.

- Risen and glorious Lord, who has ascended to appear in the presence of God on our behalf, give me the desire to worship you and the courage to be a witness to the good news you have brought to the world. Help me to do your will on earth as it is done in heaven until you come in glory. . . .

Contemplatio

Look into the face of Mary in the icon and let her serene acceptance lead you into wordless contemplative prayer.

- Spend some moments in silence praying for a spirit of joyful trust and confident expectation. Ask God to prepare your heart for the coming of the Holy Spirit.

Operatio

Consider ways that you would like to act on your experience of God's word today. Let the word of God lead you to fuller discipleship.

- Your prayerful reflection gradually transforms you into a disciple sent by Jesus to embody divine love, to teach and heal, to comfort and bring peace. In what direction is the Lord sending you today?

Pentecost

Lectio

As you prepare to hear the scriptures of Pentecost, become aware of your breathing. Breathe in, asking to be filled with the presence of God's Spirit. Breathe out, letting go of your preoccupations and anxieties.

Acts 2:1–13

When the day of Pentecost had come, they were all together in one place. And suddenly from heaven there came a sound like the rush of a violent wind, and it filled the entire house where they were sitting. Divided tongues, as of fire, appeared among them, and a tongue rested on each of them. All of them were filled with the Holy Spirit and began to speak in other languages, as the Spirit gave them ability.

Now there were devout Jews from every nation under heaven living in Jerusalem. And at this sound the crowd gathered and was bewildered, because each one heard them speaking in the native language of each. Amazed and astonished, they asked, "Are not all these who are speaking Galileans? And how is it that we hear, each of us, in our own native language? Parthians, Medes, Elamites, and residents of Mesopotamia, Judea and Cappadocia, Pontus and Asia, Phrygia and Pamphylia, Egypt and the parts of Libya belonging to Cyrene, and visitors from Rome, both Jews and proselytes, Cretans and Arabs—in our own languages we hear them speaking about God's deeds of power." All were amazed and perplexed, saying to one another, "What does this mean?" But others sneered and said, "They are filled with new wine."

The event of Pentecost, in which the Church burst forth with divine life, is narrated in just a few verses. But the significance of this occurrence is the empowerment of the disciples by the Holy Spirit, and the results of it continue throughout the Acts of the Apostles and into the third millennium. The baptism of the Church with the fire of the Spirit stirs into flame the grace of Christ's death and resurrection and breathes divine power into the newborn Church.

The descent of the Holy Spirit is described by Luke in ways that demonstrate its parallels to the Jewish feast. Pentecost, which brought pilgrims to Jerusalem from throughout the world, recalled the giving of the Torah to Israel at Mount Sinai. As God established the covenant at the mountain fifty days after the Passover lambs were sacrificed in Egypt, so now God establishes the Church in the upper room fifty days after the Lamb of God was sacrificed on the cross. As God descended on Mount Sinai with a terrifying noise and in a mysterious fire (Ex 19:16–19), so now God's Spirit descends in Jerusalem with the astonishing signs of fire and a loud sound like violent winds. At the new Pentecost, the descent of the Holy Spirit makes a new beginning in salvation history, the birth of the Church as the universal People of God.

The broad sweep of nationalities—from the east, west, north, and south—foreshadows the universality of the Christian mission. Sin has divided humanity, as expressed in the account of the tower of Babel, resulting in countless languages, separation, and misunderstanding. Pentecost prefigures the future unity of humanity as each person in the international crowd hears the apostles speaking in their own language.

Luke's gospel began with the Holy Spirit overshadowing Mary to bring forth Christ into the world; here Luke's Acts begins with the same Spirit coming upon the apostles to bring forth the Church. As the Spirit formed the physical body of Christ within Mary's womb, now that Spirit forms the mystical body of Christ, the Spirit-conceived Church. The people were amazed and perplexed, and they asked one another, "What does this mean?" The remainder of the Acts of the Apostles expresses the meaning of Pentecost as it unfolds the story of the Spirit-led mission of the Church, a story in which each of us has a part as people baptized and confirmed in the Holy Spirit.

Visio

All were amazed and perplexed upon seeing the event at Pentecost and said to one another, "What does this mean?" Gaze upon the icon to ponder its mystery so that you can better understand its meaning and deepen your desire to share in the Church's mission.

The icon of the feast of Pentecost is known as the Descent of the Holy Spirit. At the top is the familiar semicircle expressing the presence of God. The single ray of light for each of the twelve gathered expresses the movement of the Holy Spirit coming down upon the assembly. The fire of the Spirit rests upon each of them, empowering them with the Spirit's supernatural gifts. Unlike the icon of the Ascension, showing the disciples confused and disordered, here they are portrayed united together, seated in a semicircle with a halo on the head of each.

The central seat, the place of honor between Peter and Paul, seems empty. It is the seat in which Christ should be seated, but he has ascended to heaven in glory. Yet he told his disciples before his departure that he would leave them physically and send the Holy Spirit. So the icon portrays the unity of the Church, sustained by the Spirit, and surrounding Christ, who is invisibly present.

The icon expresses not just a historical event, but also the present and eternal reality of the Church. The Holy Spirit always fills the Church and anoints its ministers. The icon depicts not the historical twelve apostles, but the most significant figures of the apostolic Church. Peter is on the left and Paul on the right. Matthew, Mark, Luke, and John are there, holding books, representing the four gospels that they wrote under the inspiration of the Spirit. Likewise we see the other writers of the New Testament holding scrolls: Peter, Paul, James, and Jude. The figures are shown in a semicircle, rather than a full circle, so that we can be drawn into the unity and take our place as members of Christ's Church.

The diversity of people shown below in the doorway are the people from all parts of the world who are destined to receive the Gospel when it is preached by the apostles. They are the Parthians, Medes, Elamites, Cretans, Arabs, and people of Mesopotamia, Judea, Cappadocia, Pontus, Asia, Phrygia, Egypt, Libya, and Rome. They are still surrounded by darkness, but they are coming into the light as their amazement leads them to ask, "What does this mean?" Acts records that on the day of Pentecost about three thousand were baptized. People are still coming into the community of Christ's disciples from every continent on earth.

Meditatio

Ponder the Spirit-inspired scripture and icon in the context of the Spirit-guided Church. Consider how God is leading you to a deeper understanding of the Church and to a richer desire to share in its life.

- In Acts, the presence of the Holy Spirit is communicated in wind and fire; at Jesus's baptism the Spirit descends as a dove; in John's gospel Jesus breathes on his disciples to communicate his Spirit. Why does God reveal the Spirit's presence and power through the natural elements of the created world? Through what natural and sacramental symbols do you experience the Holy Spirit?

- Throughout the gospels the disciples are shown to be petty, misunderstanding, ambitious, fearful, and unbelieving. But at Pentecost they are united and ready to witness the Gospel to the world. How is this change an indication of the Spirit's transforming power?

- The place of honor in a Jewish gathering is the teacher's seat, around which the listeners sit. Why is this place empty in the icon of Pentecost? What does this element of the icon express about Christ's Church?

- What are the parallels between the icons of the annunciation, the baptism of Jesus, and Pentecost?

- Rather than include the historical twelve apostles, the icon includes the four evangelists and other writers of the New Testament. Why are these included here, even though some of them were not believers on the day of Pentecost? What does this aspect of the icon express about Christ's Church?

- The power of the Spirit worked wonders in and through the lives of the first disciples, and the Spirit has done the same in and through the lives of believers down through the ages. What wonders is the Holy Spirit working in and through believers today?

Oratio

After listening to what God has to say to you through the scripture and icon, consider what you want to say to God in response. Ask the Holy Spirit to bless you with a spirit of prayer.

- Come, Holy Spirit, everywhere present and filling all things, sanctify my heart for the glory of God's kingdom. O treasury of blessings and divine gifts, come abide in me and kindle in me the fire of your divine love. . . .

Contemplatio

When the words of your prayer begin to seem inadequate, ask the Holy Spirit to give you the ability to rest in God with wordless contemplative prayer.

- Imaging the Holy Spirit as mighty wind, gentle breath, or penetrating fire, let the Spirit fill you with grace and divine love. Trust that God's Spirit is recreating you from the inside out.

Operatio

Consider ways that you would like to act on your experience of God's word today, and make a commitment to change one aspect of your life.

- At Pentecost the Spirit took hold of the disciples with the force of a mighty wind and set them on fire with zeal for the reign of God. How can you stir up the gifts of service instilled within you by the grace of the Holy Spirit?

The Dormition of Mary

Lectio

Still your mind and heart as you prepare to listen to the inspired scriptures concerning the mystery of death and life. Let these words of John's gospel and Paul's letter lead you to a deeper trust in God's plan for your life and a fuller appreciation of your life's eternal worth.

John 11:25–27; 1 Corinthians 15:50–58

Jesus said to her, "I am the resurrection and the life. Those who believe in me, even though they die, will live, and everyone who lives and believes in me will never die. Do you believe this?" She said to him,

"Yes, Lord, I believe that you are the Messiah, the Son of God, the One coming into the world."

What I am saying, brothers and sisters, is this: flesh and blood cannot inherit the kingdom of God, nor does the perishable inherit the imperishable. Listen, I will tell you a mystery! We will not all die, but we will all be changed, in a moment, in the twinkling of an eye, at the last trumpet. For the trumpet will sound, and the dead will be raised imperishable, and we will be changed. For this perishable body must put on imperishability, and this mortal body must put on immortality. When this perishable body puts on imperishability, and this mortal body puts on immortality, then the saying that is written will be fulfilled: "Death has been swallowed up in victory."

> "Where, O death, is your victory?
> Where, O death, is your sting?"

The sting of death is sin, and the power of sin is the law. But thanks be to God, who gives us the victory through our Lord Jesus Christ.

Therefore, my beloved, be steadfast, immovable, always excelling in the work of the Lord, because you know that in the Lord your labor is not in vain.

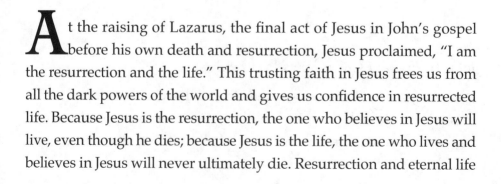

At the raising of Lazarus, the final act of Jesus in John's gospel before his own death and resurrection, Jesus proclaimed, "I am the resurrection and the life." This trusting faith in Jesus frees us from all the dark powers of the world and gives us confidence in resurrected life. Because Jesus is the resurrection, the one who believes in Jesus will live, even though he dies; because Jesus is the life, the one who lives and believes in Jesus will never ultimately die. Resurrection and eternal life are the fruit of a relationship with Jesus; wherever Jesus is, there is life that never ends.

Although we will never ultimately die because our souls will be taken to their eternal rest, we also await the day when Christ, manifested in his resurrected body, will come from heaven to raise us and transform us into his likeness. On that day of days, "we will all be changed," says Paul, both the dead and those still alive, and our perishable, mortal bodies will put on imperishability and immortality.

Although the "how" of resurrection remains a mystery, we know that God's plan for the end is not to destroy our bodies and start again but to transform our bodies, not to reject his creation but to redeem it. God's ultimate victory over sin is already assured, so that we can even today sing a taunting victory song over the fallen enemy: "Where, O death, is your victory? Where, O death, is your sting?" Death's stinging power to evoke fear, depression, and despair is already defeated through our Lord Jesus Christ. The final consequence of Christ's victory over death is stated in Paul's concluding words: "In the Lord your labor is not in vain." We can do the work of Christ with confidence, knowing that in him everything we do has ultimate meaning and eternal purpose.

Mary is the icon and model of what God will do for those who wait in faith, hope, and love. As the mother of Christ and of his disciples, Mary is the archetype and the supreme realization of our final glory. Sacred tradition and the belief of the ancient Church assure us of the glorious death and assumption of Mary, body and soul, into heaven. Rather than experience bodily corruption and await the final resurrection, Mary experienced the glorified life immediately after her death because of her singularly important role in God's plan for the world's salvation.

Visio

Let the icon of Mary's falling asleep in death draw you into the scene. Imagine standing with the apostles, who are both saddened and confident while sharing the final moments of her earthly life. Let the uncreated light of the icon illumine your heart with God's grace.

The icon of Mary's dormition commemorates her falling asleep, a Christian term for the temporary state of earthly death. The woman who welcomed the actions of God's Spirit in her life at the annunciation, the mother who trusted Jesus to bring the new wine at Cana, the woman who watched Jesus beneath the cross and was given by Jesus to be the mother of his disciples, the woman who prayed for the coming of the Holy Spirit upon the apostles continues through her death to show the way to life. She shared so intimately in the earthly life of her Son that she shared with him the experience of death and burial and was raised by him and brought to heaven to share in his glory.

Sacred tradition tells us that Mary remained in the home of John the beloved disciple in Jerusalem, continuing with the apostles the ministry of her Son in word and deed. At the time of her death, the apostles of the Lord, who were preaching throughout the world, returned to Jerusalem and gathered at her bedside. The icon shows the apostles, along with women representing the Church in Jerusalem, all focused on Mary. Peter is incensing her body while the community of disciples mourns while full of hope.

The icon is similar to that of Christ's ascension. Mary, as mother of the Church, is in the lower center. Her halo shows the grace that comes from the kingdom of God within her. Here Mary is no longer standing with raised hands but lying in death, her eyes closed and her hands crossed. Here, too, the apostles are gathered on both sides of her, while the glorified Christ dominates the upper part of the icon. Just as we look to Mary's life for our model, we look to her bodily death for hope as to where such an exemplar leads us. This hope is in eternal life, the bodily resurrection, and the new creation of the age to come.

The presence of Christ, hidden from their physical sight, is shown within the mandorla of divine glory. He is holding the holy soul of Mary in his arms. She is wrapped in a burial cloth and presented as if she were a newborn child. The parallel between Christ holding the childlike soul of Mary and the icons of Mary holding the Christ child in her own arms is an intentional reversal of roles.

Meditatio

As in the heart of Mary, God's grace within us gives us the desire to pray. Rooted in that deep desire, respond to God in prayer from your heart.

- Which words of John's gospel or Paul's letter fills you most with hope? In what ways do these words take away the sting of death?

- The victory of Christ destroys the powers of death and gives us hope and confidence in the future. Therefore, Paul urges us to "be steadfast, immovable, always excelling in the work of the Lord" because in him our labor is not in vain. How does Christ's victory lead you to do what Paul urges?

- Like those who gathered around the body of Mary, we gather around our departed loved ones and commend their souls into the hands of Christ. Remember those who have fallen asleep in the peace of Christ before us and consider the day you will be received into the new life of the age to come. How does being a member of the Communion of Saints put your life in perspective?

- An ancient hymn of the Orthodox liturgy praises Mary as "more honorable than the cherubim, and more glorious than the seraphim." The image at the top of the icon represents the six-winged seraphim, the heavenly creatures closest to God who are aflame with love for God and kindle that love in others. What assistance does this image offer to you?

- God has preserved the virginity of Mary through the conception and Nativity of Jesus, and Jesus has preserved her body from decay at her death and new life in heaven. What is the significance of Mary's virginity and bodily assumption for your own Christian faith?

- As the mother of Christ and of his disciples, Mary is the archetype and the supreme realization of our final glory. In what ways does the icon of Mary's dormition inspire you to wait in joyful hope for the coming of Jesus our Savior?

Oratio

Respond in prayer to God's word to you, imitating the trusting faith and humble acceptance of Mary. Begin with this prayer, then continue to pray in your own words.

- Lord Jesus Christ, who dwelt in the ever-virginal womb of Mary, without you our humanity is trapped in sin and destined for eternal death. Through the intercession of Mary, whom the grave could not contain, give us unshakable hope in the life of the world to come. . . .

Contemplatio

Move into wordless contemplative prayer as the words and images of prayer become no longer necessary.

- Mary shines forth on earth, until the day of the Lord comes, as a sign of sure hope for the pilgrim People of God. Place yourself in the presence of Mary your mother, accepting whatever graces God desires you to receive.

Operatio

Make a commitment to change one aspect of your life as a result of your meditation on God's word today.

- Mary is often portrayed as a model for and an expression of the Church. She is the first flowering of the Church as it will be perfected in the new creation that we await. What can you do to express devotion to Mary as you seek to be a better member of Christ's Church today?

The
Coronation of Mary

Lectio

The first text, from the books of Israel's monarchy, and the second, from the Bible's last book, lead us to a deeper understanding of God's everlasting kingdom. Ask the same Holy Spirit who inspired the sacred writers to fill your heart as you prepare to hear God's Word.

---

1 Kings 2:19–20; Revelation 11:19–12:6a

So Bathsheba went to King Solomon, to speak to him on behalf of Adonijah. The king rose to meet her, and bowed down to her; then he sat on his throne, and had a throne brought for the king's mother, and she sat on his right. Then she said, "I have one small request to make of you; do not refuse me." And the king said to her, "Make your request, my mother; for I will not refuse you."

Then God's temple in heaven was opened, and the ark of his covenant was seen within his temple; and there were flashes of lightning, rumblings, peals of thunder, an earthquake, and heavy hail.

A great portent appeared in heaven: a woman clothed with the sun, with the moon under her feet, and on her head a crown of twelve stars. She was pregnant and was crying out in birth pangs, in the agony of giving birth. Then another portent appeared in heaven: a great red dragon, with seven heads and ten horns, and seven diadems on his heads. His tail swept down a third of the stars of heaven and threw them to the earth. Then the dragon stood before the woman who was about to bear a child, so that he might devour her child as soon as it was born. And she gave birth to a son, a male child, who is to rule all the nations with a rod of iron. But her child was snatched away and taken to God and to his throne; and the woman fled into the wilderness, where she has a place prepared by God.

I n the tradition of ancient Israel, the mother of the king in the line of David received great honor. Most monarchs in the ancient world had multiple wives, but it was the king's mother who exercised the royal position as queen. She sat on a throne to the right of her son and wore a royal crown. Queen Bathsheba demonstrates the role of the queen mother as an advocate for the people as she petitions her royal son, King Solomon. Knowing that the king always listens to the intercessions of the queen mother, the people confidently make their requests to her: "Please ask King Solomon—he will not refuse you" (1 Kgs 2:17).

Fulfilling this ancient tradition, Mary is the royal mother in the kingdom of her Son. As the mother of God's Messiah, the King of Kings, she has become the queen mother of all his disciples in the kingdom of God. Because the reign of Christ, the Son of David, is universal and everlasting, so is the role of his mother. As the queen mother she serves as an advocate for us, and we can confidently make our requests to her. She lovingly presents our needs before Christ and so serves the kingdom by leading people closer to her Son. We can trust in her maternal care because she is devoted totally to our salvation.

The royal woman of Revelation, "clothed with the sun, with the moon under her feet, and on her head a crown of twelve stars," shows how the Church is embodied in Mary, the one who gives birth to her Son, destined "to rule the nations" from his place at the throne of God. The image is both the Church in its ultimate victory and also Mary, the eschatological icon of the Church. She is the archetype already enjoying the glory that the whole Church will eventually share. The glorified feminine body of Mary has joined the glorified masculine body of Jesus in the eternal kingdom of heaven.

The glorious Christ said to his Church, "Be faithful until death, and I will give you the crown of life" (Rv 2:10). Mary's faith began with a decision in Nazareth and entailed a lifetime of continual choices, changes, suffering, and growth. The humble maiden of Nazareth, through the victory of her Son and God's grace within her, has become the Mother of Mercy and the Queen of Heaven and earth.

Visio

Let the image of Mary instill in you a deep desire to share in divine life. Looking upon her with the other disciples, seek a spirit of expectant faith and joyful hope. Let this icon of heaven and earth illumine your life with God's grace.

At the annunciation, the angel greeted Mary as "full of grace." At the Visitation, Elizabeth addressed Mary as "mother of my Lord," a royal accolade for the queen mother, heard in the courts of Jerusalem and other royal cities of the ancient world. In her own canticle, Mary sang, "Surely, from now on all generations will call me blessed; for the Mighty One has done great things for me." In the Nativity, the simple maiden gave birth to the Son of God, the Lord and Savior of the world. "More honorable than the cherubim, more glorious than the seraphim," the liturgy sings her praises through the ages.

Sacred tradition tells us the holy body of Mary was carried in procession by the apostles through Jerusalem and laid in a tomb near the Garden of Gethsemane. The apostles sealed the tomb with a large stone and remained there praying and chanting psalms. Thomas the apostle was not present at the death and burial of Mary, and when he arrived late on the third day, he asked that he might be permitted to look once more upon her body to bid her farewell. When the apostles opened the tomb for him, they found there only the grave wrappings and were thus convinced of the bodily assumption. This was confirmed by the message of an angel and by her appearance to the apostles.

Centuries before the biblical books were divided into chapters, it was clearer to see how the book of Revelation introduces the "woman clothed with the sun" as the ark of the covenant in heaven. As the visionary sees the ark revealed when God's heavenly temple is opened, the heavenly woman is seen as "a great portent appeared in heaven." As the ark was the bearer of God's presence in ancient Israel, Mary is the ark of the new covenant, the eternal bearer of God's presence in her Son.

The icon shows Jesus Christ within the divine sphere of heaven, welcoming and blessing his holy mother Mary. She is shown within the mandorla, a human creature glorified and experiencing the presence of God. Her holy body was not left to the vicissitudes of the transitory world, but was incomparably exalted by its glorious ascent to heaven. The celebration of Mary's assumption into heaven and crowning as queen is a celebration of our human nature, for in Mary, human nature has reached its goal.

Meditatio

Reflect on the inspired texts and sacred icon in light of your own search for full and abundant life. Allow the scriptures and image to interact with your own world of memories, concerns, and hopes until you become aware of the personal messages the divine Word is offering to you today.

- The biblical text from the court of King Solomon describes the role of the queen mother in Israel's monarchy. In what ways does this text help you to understand the role of Mary in the kingdom of God?

- The Theotokos, the one who gave birth to God, is an ancient title of Mary. In what ways does the text of Revelation show how Mary continues in that role today and always?

- The crowning of Mary as Queen of Heaven does not make her equal to Christ her Son. Rather, as queen mother she seeks only the good of those called to God's kingdom with a deep desire to lead them to the salvation offered by her Son. In what ways does this image of Mary as queen mother help you understand her role in your life?

- Mary lives as the archetype of what God desires for every person and the great hope of our lives—the resurrection of the body and life everlasting. How does mindfulness of this goal alter your daily life?

- Mary's reign as mother of our Lord assures us that Christ hears her pleas and will not refuse her. How does this give you more confidence in your devotion to Mary and in your request for her prayers?

- In what ways has this series of icons helped illuminate God's word for you and deepened your reflection? In what ways do you wish to use sacred images in your ongoing life of prayer?

Oratio

Respond in prayer to God's word to you, imitating the trusting faith and humble acceptance of Mary. Pray in union with the angelic songs of heaven and together with the mother of the Lord. Begin with this prayer, then continue to pray in your own words.

- Son of God and Son of Mary, we pray for the coming of your kingdom on earth as it is in heaven. Help us to do the work you began among us. Inspire us to works of justice, compassion, and forgiveness until you come in glory to crown all our efforts with your eternal blessings. . . .

Contemplatio

Rest silently and confidently in the One who is the way, the truth, and the life. Trust that he will guide you into the future.

- Gaze into the face of Mary and let her maternal love lead you to her Son and to the fullness of life he offers you. Trust in her protection and know that she will beseech for you before her merciful Son.

Operatio

Consider how you will act on your experience of God's word today and determine to follow more fully in the way of discipleship.

- Consider the ways that God's grace has worked within you through these texts and icons and has transformed you from the inside. In what ways do you desire to live more fully and freely as a result of your experience of these holy mysteries of our salvation?

Stephen J. Binz is a popular Catholic speaker, biblical scholar, psychotherapist, and an award-winning author of more than forty books in biblical theology, commentary, and spirituality.

Binz, a native of Little Rock, Arkansas, earned his undergraduate degree from the University of Dallas and graduate degrees from the Pontifical Gregorian University, the Pontifical Biblical Institute in Rome and Jerusalem. He is an active member of the Society of Biblical Literature and the Catholic Biblical Association.

Binz is former director of Little Rock Scripture Study and former editor of *God's Word Today* magazine. His books include: *Scripture—God's Handbook for Evangelizing Catholics, Threshold to God's Word, Conversing with God in Scripture, Saint Peter: Flawed, Forgiven, and Faithful,* and *Panorama of the Bible.* Binz has earned three first-place awards from the Association of Catholic Publishers and also first- and second-place awards from the Catholic Press Association for his work. He often leads tours and pilgrimages to biblical lands. He and his wife, Pamela D. Pike, live in Baton Rouge, Louisiana.

Ruta and Kaspars Poikans are from Riga, Latvia, where they studied at Riga's Fine Arts Academy and School of Applied Arts. They later studied Icon painting in Russia at the Mirozka Monastery in Pskov. Since 1999, they have lived in France where they joined the Communauté du Chemin Neuf. The Poinkans make icons, frescoes, mosaics, sculptures, and liturgical furnishings in their Saint Luke Workshop at Notre Dame des Dombes Abbey.

AVE

AVE MARIA PRESS

Founded in 1865, Ave Maria Press,
a ministry of the Congregation of
Holy Cross, is a Catholic publishing
company that serves the spiritual and
formative needs of the Church and its
schools, institutions, and ministers;
Christian individuals and families; and
others seeking spiritual nourishment.

For a complete listing of titles from

Ave Maria Press

Sorin Books

Forest of Peace

Christian Classics

visit www.avemariapress.com

 AVE MARIA PRESS
AVE | Notre Dame, IN
A Ministry of the United States Province of Holy Cross